CW00767162

THINKING OUTSIDE THE BOX

Television Centre Reimagined

This book is dedicated
to the memory of
Forbes MacPherson

Contents

This is the story of a building. Not just any building, but a structure that formed one of the cornerstones of British cultural life for well over half a century. It was a building distinguished not by its architecture, although it was functional, discreet and entirely fit for purpose, but by the life and activities that happened within it.

Television Centre was a place driven by the imagination, powered by constantly changing technology and a cast of literally thousands of talented people from every sphere, all dedicated to serving the people of Britain, and beyond, with news, education, entertainment, drama, music, laughter and everyday life.

This book is also the story of a London neighbourhood, a district that has served many purposes over the span of several centuries, marking not just the relentless march of history, but the dynamics of the capital and its shifting relationship with the world. Television Centre eventually came to be a focal point of this community, but it wasn't always the case. Just as TV itself was welcomed into our homes as a means of uniting the nation, many other activities helped shape both White City and the people who came to visit, live and work here.

Today, Television Centre is both a place to live as well as a place to work and be entertained. Once the flagship structure of the BBC's sprawling property empire, it became known as the nexus of the technological revolution, broadcasting to the world. The site it stands on was the location of another symbol of global togetherness, a series of celebratory international exhibitions running from 1908 to 1914. Close by was the White City Stadium, which ultimately ended its days as a greyhound racing track. Yet it was originally built as the primary venue for the 1908 Olympic Games, the 'Games of the IV Olympiad', the first of three to be held in London (and also the longest Olympic competition in history, running for over six months). It was a forerunner of all modern stadiums, and a place where Olympic history was forged.

When the sale of Television Centre was finally confirmed in 2012 after four years of speculation – all part of a broad restructuring of the BBC's portfolio and annual budgets – there was an entirely understandable outcry from broadcasters, viewers and the talent themselves, many of whom had spent a large proportion of their working lives in and around the sprawling complex. At Television Centre's peak, some 6,000 people called it their main place of work. It produced live broadcasts that regularly attracted audiences in the tens of millions, almost unthinkable numbers in the modern era of fragmented, multichannel viewing. The building's seven studios (albeit not all dedicated to the BBC's own output by the time the building was sold) were responsible for thousands of hours of television every year, a significant proportion of the Corporation's annual output. From its central circular courtyard, Thomas Bayliss Huxley-Jones' golden sculpture of the Greek sun god Helios symbolised television being broadcast – as light – around the world.

Television Centre, viewed from
Wood Lane, 2014.

Times had changed. By 2011, the BBC was said to own 585,000 square metres of property in the UK (about 6.3 million square feet). Its 483 locations ranged from administrative buildings and storage depots through to small local radio stations, recording complexes, theatres, countless stores, offices, rehearsal rooms, workshops and technical facilities. Over its 90-year history, the BBC had had key buildings dotted across London in prime locations, from Broadcasting House on Portland Place, to Bush House (home of the World Service), the recording studios at Maida Vale, Lime Grove and Alexandra Palace, not to mention the iconic Television Theatre, the original Shepherd's Bush Empire, built in 1903. There was also the BBC Overseas Broadcasting Service at Aldenham House, the studio complexes at Riverside, Ealing and Elstree, the latter run by the BBC since 1983, as well as the Paris Theatre and the Hippodrome Theatre and numerous temporary offices scattered around the capital.

Although some of these locations had already come and gone, the Corporation's move to MediaCity UK in Salford in 2011 was undertaken not just to consolidate the sprawling empire, but to broaden its relationship with the nation and undo decades of perceived London-centric bias. That same year, the BBC received £3.6bn in licence fees, fuelling a creativity mill that needed careful fiscal management.

An aerial view of the Television Centre site, 2014. The sprawling complex occupied 14 acres of land to the west of Wood Lane and at its peak was the workplace for more than 6,000 BBC staff.

So how did so much of our collective cultural memory become so inextricably bound up with a few acres of land in West London? It's hard to overstate the ubiquitous presence of Television Centre in our lives. Although for the most part, viewers only saw the austere curved façade on Wood Lane, the implication was that of a 24-hour factory of culture, a place where familiar faces and famous names stood alongside an army of technicians and support staff. It was a place where screaming teenagers pursued nervous pop stars, where general elections were deciphered and declared, where the news of the day was brought vividly to life, and where telethons and charity events played out in full view of the public, as well as on our screens.

As Television Centre played its pivotal role over 50 years, White City was changing around it. Railway yards gave way to industrial warehouses during the post-war years, before they were in turn replaced by some of Europe's most substantial retail spaces in the early 21st century. New offices and apartments – the first residences to be developed in White City for over 30 years – have been joined by bars, cafés and restaurants that are a far cry from the BBC's legendary canteens.

This book is a chronicle of that change, a document of modern London. Underpinning it all are the memories of our relationship with culture, and how Television Centre's history lives on for new generations.

NO SMOKING

The history of London W12

In the pre-railway age, a traveller to the far-flung reaches of West London would have left the grand avenues and parks of the city behind and be walking down small country lanes, past open fields and farms, criss-crossed by ancient paths, common land, mills and homesteads. Modernity came in the form of the main arterial roads that linked the capital to Oxford and beyond, but even after the coming of the train during the great 'Railway Mania' of the 1840s, an area like Notting Hill was still rural enough to have space for the short-lived Kensington Hippodrome, a racecourse designed to rival Epsom.

It couldn't last. Railways brought industry, and industry demanded labour. New territories opened up this land to speculation, and London expanded, with farms and fields swiftly consumed by the march of the factory and the house builder. Some areas changed faster than others. The character of an area like Shepherd's Bush was still largely untouched after the first tranche of rail lines were laid down, and by the mid-nineteenth century, a Londoner could still walk the four miles from the hustle and bustle of the West End to find themselves amongst the relative peace and quiet of a common like Wormwood Scrubs. If they then turned south, along Wood Lane, they'd pass Hoof's Farm, Wormholt Farm and Wood Lane Farm, their fields bisected by the new brick viaducts of the Hammersmith and City Line, before eventually joining up with the Uxbridge Road.

As the farms left, developers moved in to build housing, but significant open spaces remained. Rail depots, generating stations and factories started to imprint an industrial character on the area, while the military character of Wormwood Scrubs – designated a 'metropolitan exercising ground' for cavalry, as well as being open to the public – was bolstered by the creation of the famous prison, opened in 1891. The railway changed the tone and character of West London forever. Shepherd's Bush, believed to be named for its role as a gathering space for livestock and their drivers en route to the markets at Smithfield, was given a station in 1900. In the decade that followed, the patch of open ground was a hive of activity, eventually becoming fringed by homes, churches and theatres, including the opening of the Shepherd's Bush Empire in 1903.

Above: Wormwood Scrubs prison, built in 1891.

Below: Shepherd's Bush station, on the Central London Railway, opened in 1900.

In 1908, the open land between Wormwood Scrubs and Shepherd's Bush was bestowed a new name, one that was alien and entirely unrelated to the centuries of history that had shaped these city fringes. The Franco-British Exhibition and the 1908 London Olympics literally put White City on the map, the name referencing the glowing white stucco of the exhibition's many and varied pavilions. The exhibition was paired with the Games of the IV Olympiad. Originally assigned to Rome, they had been moved to London at short notice following the 1906 eruption of Vesuvius. The Games also required venues, and a new 'Great Stadium' was built in just eight months to the designs of the engineer John James Webster, set alongside the Franco-British Exhibition's 140-acre site.

These were early years for the Olympics and for professional athletics, and it was an event still finding its role. Amongst the 22 sports being showcased were the tug-of-war and duelling with wax bullets, but amid all the anachronisms, the Great Stadium stood out. Seating 93,000 people, it featured banked seating and a strikingly modern profile and is often cited as the first truly contemporary stadium, a template for all that followed. It was also the finishing point for the 1908 Olympic Marathon, a race notable not just for its controversial ending (the winning runner, Italian Dorando Pietri, was subsequently disqualified for being helped over the finish line). With a route starting on the East Terrace at Windsor Castle and heading through Uxbridge, Ruislip, Harrow and Wembley, before crossing Wormwood Scrubs and ending in the stadium, the final distance to be run was 26 miles 385 yards. The traditional explanation for these arbitrary extra yards was the race organisers' desire for the race to finish beneath the stadium's Royal Box. The end result was that the 1908 race inadvertently set this distance in stone for every subsequent marathon event, Olympic or otherwise.

Above: the 93,000 capacity White City Stadium was designed and built in just eight months, ready for the 1908 Olympic Games.

Opposite page: scenes from the Games, which featured 22 sports and lasted over six months.

An exhausted Dorando Pietri of Italy is pictured being helped to complete the final yards of the men's marathon. He was later disqualified and first place was given to John Hayes of the USA, who set an Olympic Record of 2 hours, 55 minutes and 18 seconds.

Right: 24 July 1908 saw one of the highlights of the Games, the men's marathon. Fifty-five competitors from 16 nations began the race, with just 27 crossing the finish line (by comparison, the 2016 men's Olympic marathon had 155 starters, 140 of whom finished). The course was exactly 26 miles and 385 yards, the distance from Windsor to White City, followed by one lap of the stadium. This distance was made the standard in 1921.

Below: Eton High Street, Berkshire. The race began at Windsor Castle, which is visible in the distance.

Opposite page: divers at the White City Stadium.

THE GREAT
MARATHON RACE

Windsor Castle to the Stadium, London,

FRIDAY, JULY 24TH, 1908.

IN view of the fact that this historic Race cannot take place in this Country again for at least thirty years, and bearing in mind that Windsor has been honoured by being selected as the starting place, the Mayor makes an earnest appeal to all Shopkeepers and Employers of Labour in the District to

CLOSE THEIR PREMISES from 1 o'clock to 3.30

on the day, thereby enabling their Employees to witness the Start of what will be a striking and most interesting event in the history of our Town.

About 70 Competitors of all nations will take part in the Race.

Today's Games are massive events that require years of planning and huge investments in infrastructure. Yet in terms of scale and public interest, the adjoining Franco-British Exhibition was deemed to be of much more interest to Londoners. Over five months, the event attracted some 9 million people to visit the exhibition halls, fun rides and performances. The original idea was the suggestion of Hungarian-born impresario Imre Kiralfy, the promoter of the 1895 Empire of India Exhibition on the site of what would become the Earls Court Exhibition Centre. Kiralfy had a natural taste for spectacle and scale, and saw the commercial potential in celebrating this event with a show.

Following the signing of the Entente Cordiale on 8 April 1904, a non-aggression and co-operation agreement designed to end the regular conflicts that had defined the national histories of the two countries for centuries, he envisaged a new city set in the "barren wastes of Shepherd's Bush" (his words), that would lure Londoners west to see and experience the wonders of the world. Crucially, his vision appealed to the colonial aspirations and intentions of each power, thereby ensuring that Britain and France's desire for global reach and influence would define the content and form of the 1908 exhibition.

The 140-acre site contained 20 pavilions, each rendered in an elaborate, ornate style evolved from the casual colonial-era appropriation of different architectural forms and typologies from all around the globe. In addition there were seven exhibition halls, with displays and participants designed to showcase Imperial splendour and benevolent power. Halls were given over to British and French textiles, horticulture and modern industrial machinery and both Fine and Decorative Arts. There were also amusement rides, including the Spiral, Flip Flap and Toboggan rides, along with the impressive Canadian Scenic Railway, a proto-roller coaster that took sightseers up and around an artificial mountain range.

Below: crowds at the Franco-British Exhibition, held between May and October 1908, in the newly built 'White City'. The spectacle attracted over 8 million people.

Opposite page: a postcard from the event celebrates the Entente Cordiale, an agreement of peace and co-operation signed between Britain and France four years earlier.

The 1908 Franco-British Exhibition occupied a 140-acre site to the north of Shepherd's Bush and featured 20 immaculate white pavilions, along with landscaped gardens and amusement rides. The hugely successful event was the design of Hungarian-born Imre Kiralfy, who went on to orchestrate five more exhibitions during the following decade.

L.S.& P.Cº.

On the Lagoon, Franco-British Exhibition, London, 1908

FRANCO   BRITISH

(AS SHE IS SPOKEN)

IF "AMOUR" MEANS "LOVE," WHEN I'M ASKING OF THEE,
DO YOU LOVE ME, SWEET ONE, LET YOUR ANSWER BE "OUI."

TOM EDWARDS.   COPYRIGHT.   LONDON.

This page: postcards from the 1908 Franco-British Exhibition.

Opposite page: the Flip Flap amusement ride, over 200 feet tall, with another ride, the Wiggle Waggle, on the left.

One night I lay awake in bed and, as if by magic, I saw stretched out in my mind's eye, an imposing city of palaces, domes and towers, set in cool, green spaces and intersected by many bridged canals.

But it had one characteristic, which made it strangely beautiful. Hitherto I had dealt in colour in the shimmering hues of gold and silver. This city was spotlessly white. I saw it all in an instant, and the next day I had jotted down the scheme of what London was to know as the 'White City'.

Imre Kiralfy, *My Reminiscences.*
First published in *The Strand Magazine* in
1909, reproduced in the Exhibition Study
Group, Journal No. 64, Spring 2002.

This photograph was taken from the top of the 'Flip Flap' amusement ride and shows the scale of the site. The exhibition's size and colour bestowed the new name 'White City' on this previously undeveloped area of West London.

I was so tired after doing the rounds at the Exhibition!

This was the very height of Empire. Canada, Australia and New Zealand were prominently represented by grandiose individual pavilions, and a large central lagoon was flanked by promenades, bandstands and restaurants. There were 'village' displays of vernacular architecture and local residents from Ceylon, India and Senegal, all transported to West London for the curious amusement of Edwardian Londoners. The crowds were well served by the new Central Line station at Wood Lane, which opened the same day as the exhibition, and there were special rail and sea services from France. The 'Great White City' exhibition was a financial success as well as being a spectacular display, well received by critics and public alike.

For many people, White City was the only representation of Empire – and therefore the world at large – that they had ever seen. What had once been little more than hinterland had been transformed into a window on the world. The coming war was to bring not just unimaginable destruction but also massive change, and hindsight tends to rob the moment of its power. It was also a time of rapid technological change, barely five years after the first powered flight, with railways above and below ground transforming the speed of travel, and the new field of radio showing promise. Nearby Wormwood Scrubs became one of the haunts of Britain's earliest aviators, fearless men like Claude Graham-White, John Moore-Brabazon and Charles Rolls. An open expanse of flat land, it provided the space to exercise the unpredictable canvas and wood contraptions that pioneers would hurl into the sky, demonstrating speed and aerobatics, as well as well-publicised races across the nation. The Scrubs eventually became home to an airship shed, paid for and proudly sponsored by the *Daily Mail*, and for a while this incongruous symbol of the new century sat alone on the fields.

Machinery and technology was an integral part of the era's exhibition culture. The Franco-British Exhibition was by no means the first of these shows, for it continued a long and illustrious tradition started by the Great Exhibition of 1851 and followed by world's fairs and international exhibitions around the globe. Kiralfy simply transformed the grandiose ideal into a commercial venture. Having established the infrastructure on the site, five other fairs followed, starting with the Imperial International Exhibition of 1909.

In 1910, White City hosted the Japan-British Exhibition, a huge display that supported the Anglo-Japanese Alliance signed in 1902. Intended to promote Japanese culture and industry with displays of manufactured goods, and craft, it also included meticulously recreated Japanese gardens (a small part of which survives in the present-day Hammersmith Park where it meets Frithville Gardens), while the Canadian railroad became the Japanese mountain railway. The Flip Flap ride was retained, with its twin steel arms swinging back and forth as they raised passengers up to 200 feet in the air. Although these rather more populist elements were frowned upon by the Japanese press, who didn't consider the exhibition a success, the event still brought many more millions to White City.

Above and opposite: images from the Japan-British Exhibition held in 1910. Following the success of the Franco-British Exhibition two years earlier, this second huge display attracted millions more to White City. Part of the Japanese gardens survive to this day in Hammersmith Park.

The following year, 1911, with the site still overseen by Kiralfy, it hosted the Coronation Exhibition to mark the crowning of King George V, before it focused on yet another part of the globe with the Latin-British Exhibition of 1912. Kiralfy's final exhibition on the site, curtailed by the First World War and the end of this fertile period of international collaboration, was the Anglo-American Exhibition of 1914. Visitors could walk through scale models of Manhattan and the Grand Canyon, together with bustling sideshows and rides inspired by Coney Island and Bostock's Circus, with the whirring of machinery blending with the sounds of bands and the roars of lions bouncing off the ornate façades.

Kiralfy was to die in Brighton in 1919, exhausted by a lifetime of translating urban and cultural evolution into overnight spectacles. The White City faded fast, and the buildings, never designed for permanent use, were given over to temporary manufacturing, storage and training spaces during the First World War. The stadium fared rather better, as we'll see, but the exhibition site was eventually completely abandoned, its funfair rides rusted and dormant, with overgrown vegetation obscuring the once pristine façades of the exhibition halls.

Following the First World War, Kiralfy's exhibition site fell into decline. However, several slightly less glamorous events continued to be held in White City throughout the 1920s and 30s, such as the International Advertising Exhibition and the British Industries Fair.

Demolition of the Haunted House
amusement ride, a remnant of the
White City exhibition site, 1937.
Following years of abandonment,
the site was cleared to make way
for social housing.

It was time for a new chapter. A few years earlier, half a mile to the west, Wormholt Farm had become the Wormholt Estate, the first foray into the large-scale residential projects that were to completely transform the area. In 1935, a substantial proportion of the now derelict White City, around 52 acres, was bought by the London County Council. The White City Estate was finally completed after 1945, housing nearly 9,000 people in 35 blocks. Its high density was a response to the capital's pressing need for housing, and a rejection of the more picturesque 'garden city' style planning that originally characterised municipal housing schemes. The estate's accommodation was relatively high specification, with balconies, central courtyards, fitted kitchens and bathrooms, and dedicated chutes for rubbish from the upper levels. The central spine was renamed Commonwealth Avenue, and the new blocks were arranged around roads that reflected the site's history: Australia Road, Canada Way, India Way.

Despite the quality, the uniform appearance of the estate was criticised, even though the green space quota (including Hammersmith Park, which reused part of the Japanese Garden) was high and the facilities good. Over time, White City's fortunes and reputation declined, and while the estate has been the focus of renewal and change over the past decade, one struggles to evoke the sights and sounds that must have thronged the site over a century ago.

Below: workers dismantling the Flip Flap ride, to make way for the new housing estate, 1937.

Opposite page: an extract from the County of London Plan by JH Forshaw and Patrick Abercrombie, published in 1943. The article details the construction of the White City Estate, which had begun in 1936 before being halted by the outbreak of war in 1939. The site was eventually completed in 1945.

1. AIR VIEW OF THE WHITE CITY HOUSING ESTATE, HAMMERSMITH

This is the largest estate developed by the London County Council with blocks of flats; commenced in 1936, work was suspended in September, 1939. It occupies an area of about 52 acres and, if completed as planned, will comprise 49, 5-storey blocks of flats with accommodation for 11,000 people.

N.B.—Modification may, however, be considered as to the number and height of the blocks still to be built.

Site reservations have been made for the future construction of a community centre, shops, two schools, churches and other public buildings.

E. P. Wheeler, F.R.I.B.A., Architect to the Council, and F. R. Hiorns, F.R.I.B.A. J. W. Hepburn, F.R.I.B.A., Assistant Architect.

2. BANBURY HOUSE, PENSHURST ROAD
Typical example of flats erected by the Council during 1935-1938.

The 'Great White City' demonstrated that urbanism and culture could be combined with the magic of spectacle to create a commercially viable space that was neither a traditional city, nor a dedicated performance space. It's something we accept without question today, in an era of shopping as entertainment, when retail spaces span whole city blocks and commercial architecture is carefully imagineered to keep us engaged. The pioneers behind the White City exhibitions, and to a lesser extent the Olympics of 1908, understood the importance of place and memory in the modern city, a characteristic that was inevitably lost in its transition to housing estate.

Our sense of spectacle has also changed. The grand Edwardian exhibitions were obviously products of their age, with the casual racism of their colonial displays (in particular the 'villages') and the innate belief in the superiority of Empire. Over just six years from 1908, White City was to provide Londoners with an insight into the world around them, albeit one filtered through the lens of colonialism. What came next, however, would present the world in a very different way. The broadcasting era would deliver unimaginable change, forever altering the nature of the world. Rather than bring the world to W12, the new technologies of radio and television promised to deliver it right into your home.

The Court of Honour, one of 20 pavilions that formed the Franco-British Exhibition of 1908. The pristine white buildings had been host to millions of visitors and gave the area its new name: 'White City'. However, the site was eventually demolished and today few traces survive.

The beginnings of the BBC

This book is not a history of the BBC, nor should it be. Yet the Corporation's history and legacy has become an integral part of this London neighbourhood. The story of how the BBC came to create a piece of architecture that would ultimately come to define it – as an institution, as a physical space and as a cultural force for the UK and the world – is also the story of broadcasting itself.

Television Centre was not the first headquarters of the Corporation, of course, for the BBC had already been integral in the establishment of the technology known as television. Like many fundamental human inventions, television didn't arrive fully formed. For a decade or so from the mid-1920s, inventors were effectively chasing the dead end of 'mechanical' television. This labour-intensive approach to transmitting moving pictures, involving a perforated disc that would rotate to generate the video signal, was the culmination of many different theories and experiments, eventually distilled into a functional working prototype by the Scotsman John Logie Baird. Baird receives – and deserves – much of the credit for popularising the idea of television and proving there was a market. As a technologist he was so ahead of his time that he was experimenting with workable colour and HD systems in the 1940s, decades before they became mainstream, yet his original mechanical system rapidly became obsolete as electronic scanning methods, such as the cathode ray tube, came to the fore.

The British Broadcasting Company was established on 18 October 1922, becoming the British Broadcasting Corporation on 1 January 1927. The Company's General Manager, John Reith, became the first Director General. The BBC's television service made experimental transmissions from 1930 onwards, largely to compare Baird's system to the higher-definition process known as Marconi-EMI. The Corporation carried programmes made by Baird's own Baird Television Development Company, but the technology proved unwieldy and less agile than that found at its own studios at Alexandra Palace.

Top: John Logie Baird, pictured in 1942 with one of his early television projectors. Baird had successfully pioneered the transmission of images in the late 1920s and is widely credited as the inventor of television.

Above: Lord John Charles Walsham Reith, who served as the first Director General of the British Broadcasting Corporation from its inception in 1927 until 1938.

Opposite page: DG Birkinshaw
operating an early Marconi-EMI
camera outside the BBC's television
studios at Alexandra Palace, North
London, 1936.

Below: the BBC's European Service
control room, 1943. During the war
the BBC focused its attention on
radio broadcasts; widespread public
adoption of television did not occur
until the 1950s.

Broadcasting House

The original BBC Headquarters building was designed in 1932 by the architects George Valentine S Myer and FJ Watson-Hart. Located in the heart of London's West End, it had a curved Portland stone façade that matched the grand terraces of the surrounding Portland Estate. The building still stands today, as BBC Broadcasting House. Its ten-year, £1bn refurbishment, completed in 2013, involved restoration, extension and the consolidation of an entire block, creating a landmark structure that rises up above its surroundings like the prow of a modern ocean liner. Originally, Myer and Watson-Hart designed the building to be a striking counterpoint to John Nash's All Souls Church on Langham Place (1824), adorning this temple of broadcasting with murals and sculptures, including notable work by Eric Gill. Inside, the studios were fitted out by some of the most progressive designers of the 1930s (although their work was short-lived in the fast-moving world of broadcast technology), including Raymond McGrath, Serge Chermayeff and Wells Coates.

Although the BBC's television coverage began an official regular service in 1936 from Alexandra Palace, the outbreak of war in 1939 abruptly curtailed the development of both programming and technology. Throughout this period, Broadcasting House and its radio output was the Corporation's focal point, especially in the war years, during which time it was bombed twice, once live on air, with a total loss of eight lives. As an essential component of the war effort, radio provided vital (albeit carefully censored) news, boosting morale with entertainment and providing guidance and instruction to the nation. While newspapers and newsreels provided frequently unsettling imagery of the war, radio was the voice of the nation. Television's era had yet to come.

Above: artist Eric Gill at work on his sculpture *Ariel Between Wisdom and Gaiety* that decorates the exterior of Broadcasting House.

Below: Prime Minister Winston Churchill pictured in 1943 addressing the British public via BBC radio from the White House in Washington, DC.

Opposite page: the BBC's purpose-built headquarters on Portland Place, London W1. The building was officially opened in May 1932.

The Second World War saw a seven-year cessation of television development and broadcasting. The BBC started television transmissions again on 7 June 1946, with the continuity announcers acting as if almost nothing had happened. These were pioneering years in television technology. In the early 1950s the BBC outgrew the facilities at Alexandra Palace and moved television to studio facilities in Lime Grove, near Shepherd's Bush. These had previously served as the Gaumont Film Studios and dated back to 1915, making them some of the earliest purpose-built film studios in the country.

Broadcasting architecture had to be flexible and adaptable, not least because of rapid evolution of every facet of broadcasting technology. The BBC's acquisition of Lime Grove was initially a stopgap, but the facilities continued to play a key role in BBC TV production for many decades to come. At around the same time, in 1953, the Corporation bought the Shepherd's Bush Empire. It became the BBC Television Theatre. Both sites were close to White City, by then a sprawling, partly derelict complex of buildings that had housed wartime manufacturing and logistics. A substantial chunk of the original exhibition site had been given over to Local Authority housing, but the BBC took a 14-acre plot for the next stage in its history. The goal was to create the ultimate dedicated centre for television production, a tailor-made space that would house the burgeoning technology and all the ancillary administration, technology and management accompanying its production.

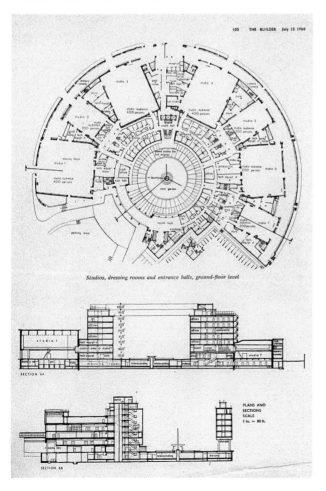

WHITE CITY

BROADCASTING CORPORATION   WHITE CITY SITE   PROPOSED TELEVISION DEVELOPMENT

Plan of the projected Radio Centre at WHITE CITY, London.
The new Television Headquarters is in black.

100   THE BUILDER   July 15 1960

Studios, dressing rooms and entrance halls, ground-floor level

SECTION AA

SECTION BB

PLANS AND
SECTIONS
SCALE
1 in. = 80 ft.

Opposite page: architect Graham
Dawbarn (left) and civil engineer
Marmaduke Tudsbery (right) inspect
a scale model of their Television
Centre design. This model was
prepared for display at the Festival
of Britain, 1951.

Left: original drawings from the
development of the scheme show
its unique 'question mark' design
and circular inner courtyard.

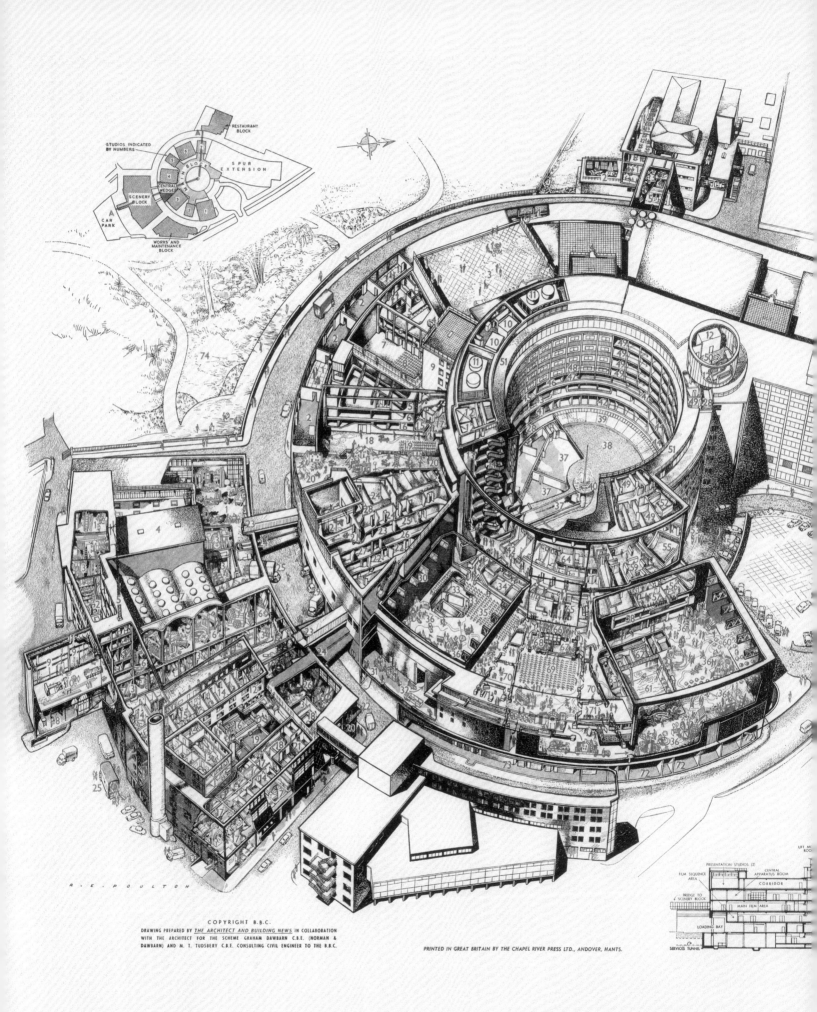

STUDIOS INDICATED
BY NUMBERS

RESTAURANT
BLOCK

NEW BLOCK

SPUR
EXTENSION

CENTRAL
WEDGE

SCENERY
BLOCK

CAR
PARK

WORKS' AND
MAINTENANCE
BLOCK

PRESENTATION STUDIOS (2)

FILM SEQUENCE
AREA

CENTRAL
APPARATUS ROOM

CORRIDOR

BRIDGE TO
SCENERY BLOCK

MAIN FILM AREA

LOADING BAY

SERVICES TUNNEL

A·E·POULTON

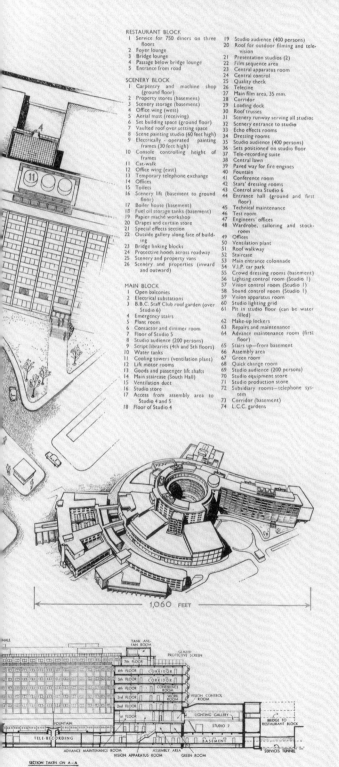

B.B.C. TELEVISION CENTRE
Impression of the buildings, now under construction in London

RESTAURANT BLOCK
1 Service for 750 diners on three floors
2 Foyer lounge
3 Bridge lounge
4 Passage below bridge lounge
5 Entrance from road

SCENERY BLOCK
1 Carpentry and machine shop (ground floor)
2 Property stores (basement)
3 Scenery storage (basement)
4 Office wing (west)
5 Aerial mast (receiving)
6 Set building space (ground floor)
7 Vaulted roof over setting space
8 Scene painting studio (60 feet high)
9 Electrically - operated painting frames (30 feet high)
10 Console controlling height of frames
11 Cat-walk
12 Office wing (east)
13 Temporary telephone exchange
14 Offices
15 Toilets
16 Scenery lift (basement to ground floor)
17 Boiler house (basement)
18 Fuel oil storage tanks (basement)
19 Papier maché workshop
20 Drapes and curtain store
21 Special effects section
22 Outside gallery along face of building
23 Bridge linking blocks
24 Protective hoods across roadway
25 Scenery and property vans
26 Scenery and properties (inward and outward)

MAIN BLOCK
1 Open balconies
2 Electrical substations
3 B.B.C. Staff Club roof garden (over Studio 6)
4 Emergency stairs
5 Plant room
6 Contactor and dimmer room
7 Floor of Studio 5
8 Studio audience (200 persons)
9 Script libraries (4th and 5th floors)
10 Water tanks
11 Cooling towers (ventilation plant)
12 Lift motor rooms
13 Goods and passenger lift shafts
14 Main staircase (South Hall)
15 Ventilation duct
16 Studio store
17 Access from assembly area to Studio 4 and 5
18 Floor of Studio 4

19 Studio audience (400 persons)
20 Roof for outdoor filming and television
21 Presentation studios (2)
22 Film sequence area
23 Central apparatus room
24 Central control
25 Quality check
26 Telecine
27 Main film area, 35 mm.
28 Corridor
29 Loading dock
30 Roof trusses
31 Scenery runway serving all studios
32 Scenery entrance to studio
33 Echo effects rooms
34 Dressing rooms
35 Studio audience (400 persons)
36 Sets positioned on studio floor
37 Tele-recording suite
38 Central lawn
39 Paved way for fire engines
40 Fountain
41 Conference room
42 Stars' dressing rooms
43 Control area Studio 6
44 Entrance hall (ground and first floor)
45 Technical maintenance
46 Test room
47 Engineers' offices
48 Wardrobe, tailoring and stock-room
49 Offices
50 Ventilation plant
51 Roof walkway
52 Staircase
53 Main entrance colonnade
54 V.I.P. car park
55 Crowd dressing rooms (basement)
56 Lighting control room (Studio 1)
57 Vision control room (Studio 1)
58 Sound control room (Studio 1)
59 Vision apparatus room
60 Studio lighting grid
61 Pit in studio floor (can be water filled)
62 Make-up lockers
63 Repairs and maintenance
64 Advance maintenance room (first floor)
65 Stairs up—from basement
66 Assembly area
67 Green room
68 Quick change room
69 Studio audience (200 persons)
70 Studio equipment store
71 Studio production store
72 Subsidiary rooms—telephone system
73 Corridor (basement)
74 L.C.C. gardens

1,060 FEET

SECTION TAKEN ON A-A

With this in mind, the architect Graham Dawbarn was appointed in November 1949. Dawbarn, who co-founded the office of Norman and Dawbarn in 1934 with Squadron Leader (later Air Commodore) Nigel Norman, was best known as a designer for another nascent high-technology industry, civil aviation. Norman and Dawbarn had set out the basic form of some of the UK's principal airports, including Gatwick, Birmingham and Manchester. Birmingham Airport's Elmdon terminal, designed by the firm, still stands, a bold modern structure with a tier of semi-circular balconies rising up above the airfield. Norman was killed on active service on 1943, having spent his wartime service requisitioning – and enhancing – airports for RAF use. Dawbarn continued in private practice; the BBC commission was to occupy the next 11 years of his life. His BBC counterpart was Marmaduke Tudsbery, a former Royal Engineer who had worked for the BBC since 1925. Tudsbery served as the Corporation's Consulting Civil Engineer, and from 1949 onwards the rest of his career revolved around the Television Centre commission.

From the outset, it was intended to be distinct from the pre-war authoritarianism of Broadcasting House, both in aesthetic and approach. Like many of the world's great buildings, Television Centre has its own origin myth. The spiralling shape of the building, with the studio complexes radiating out from the splinter-like statue of Helios at the centre of the Rotunda, was reportedly based on the shape of the question mark. And not just any question mark, but one squiggled on the back of the proverbial envelope by Dawbarn himself at an early design meeting. Whether the doodle inspired the design or was simply a visual expression of Dawbarn's concept has been lost to time, but the story remains a favourite and neat summation of Television Centre's final form. In fact, the idea of a ring of studios had existed since the early days of film, partly to speed up production by rotating heavy camera equipment between pre-built scenes and to maximise the use of natural sunlight. Dawbarn's firm also favoured the circular form as it was a natural shape for aviation architecture (his unbuilt plan for Heathrow Airport took a similar form), and his stripped-back approach to detail, decoration and materials conveyed just the right mix of official gravitas and abstemious use of public money.

A detailed cut-away drawing of Television Centre, prepared by Dawbarn and Tudsbery for *The Architect and Building News*, July 1958. The staggering level of detail indicates how the vast 'factory for television' would operate its seven studios and countless supporting facilities.

Construction and opening

Although building work began in 1950 it was almost immediately halted for a few years due to ongoing restrictions on materials, caused in part by the outbreak of the Korean War in June that year. The contractor was Higgs & Hill, a family-owned building company that had worked on BBC contracts since the early 1930s, including at Broadcasting House, Crystal Palace and Maida Vale. Work recommenced in 1953, with the Scenery Block the first structure to be completed and made operational in early 1954. This building was also home to an impressive boiler house and the power control. The central office structure wasn't started until March 1955 and construction concluded five years later. Television Centre was the largest television studio complex in Europe when it opened on 29 June 1960.

The finished building contained 12 TV studios, eight large and four small, along with a number of smaller studios for news and weather bulletins. The huge site allowed the structure to sprawl for tens of thousands of square feet, despite its modest seven-storey height. The basement spaces alone spread for some three and a half acres, while 85 dressing rooms catered for over 600 performers at a time. Peter Bax, the BBC's first Television Design Manager, parlayed his considerable experience from other fields, including his time as a stage manager at Drury Lane Theatre. Bax was instrumental in reshaping the BBC's film and theatre spaces for television production. Pre-war TV had been live, meaning that sets had to be changed as swiftly and silently as any theatre production, and shared many of the same skillsets and requirements in carpentry, engineering and lighting. Bax's experience and recommendations were to be central to the brief for the new dedicated Television Centre. Together with Tudsbery and Dawbarn, Bax's experience ensured that the BBC's requirements for the new building were sophisticated and to the very highest standard.

63

Above: the completed Television Centre complex, photographed from Hammersmith Park in June 1960. The circular 'doughnut' stands tall in the centre, with the surrounding ring of seven studios encircling the base.

Left, top: the canteen block was one of the first elements of the site to be completed, pictured here in 1956.

Left, bottom: the scenery block had been completed even earlier, in 1953. The barrel-vaulted concrete roof featured distinctive round perforated ceiling lights, which were said to be one of the inspirations for the design of the Daleks in *Doctor Who*.

The iconic façade of Television Centre, photographed from the Wood Lane approach in 1962. The building remained in this form for just a few years before more facilities were required; the empty space on the right-hand side of this image was filled by the Spur extension, which was completed in 1969.

Left: the Helios statue, designed
by TB Huxley-Jones, stands
proudly above the fountain at the
centre of the circular courtyard,
photographed in 1961. The ancient
Greek sun god is joined by two
smaller sculptures at the base of
the fountain which represent sound
and vision.

Above: Her Majesty Queen
Elizabeth II pictured with Kenneth
Adam, Director of Television
Broadcasting for the BBC, as
she toured the newly opened
Television Centre complex in 1961.

From the day it opened, refurbishments and additions were a constant fact of life at Television Centre, with the studios themselves undergoing near-constant change. The endless cycle of programme making required constant movement and activity. A programme would involve the building of sets, rigging and lighting, then rehearsals and finally filming, either for live or later broadcast. The studio would then be 'struck', or dismantled, so that the next programme could be made. By the 1980s, a typical day for Studio 7, for example, would begin in the early hours with the BBC's breakfast programme, followed by *Newsround*, and finally by *Newsnight* before the breakfast set was installed for the following day and the whole cycle began again. Between each filming session, an army of technicians would appear to take down and reassemble the studio.

The technical spaces were a crucial part of Television Centre's culture and ethos. As well as production offices for news, drama, documentary and light entertainment, the building was originally built to house the BBC's design department, located above the scenery block at the rear of the building. In the days before independent production companies, everyone was in-house, from the canteen and cleaning staff all the way up to the Director General, creating a unique atmosphere and sense of togetherness. The newness of the space and the growing prestige and popularity of television also created a different dynamic. Former employees noted that the atmosphere in both Broadcasting House and Maida Vale was considered rather old-fashioned and genteel compared to the aggressive, dynamic environment of Television Centre.

The formative years of television were an incalculably valuable cultural legacy. Yet although TV's intense cultural importance was clear almost immediately, it was also a heartbreakingly ephemeral medium, just as radio had been at the outset. Thousands of hours of early radio and television broadcasts, once they had been consumed by their clustered audiences, were never to be repeated. Plays were performed as if to an invisible audience of thousands, orchestras filled the early studios and played live, setting up the systems and rituals of broadcasting that continue today. Yet once these broadcasts were sent off into the ether they were gone forever. By 1932, when Broadcasting House was opened, it was discovered that there were practically no recordings at all from the first decade of BBC Radio. Recordings were only made – usually to vinyl disc or cylinder – to preserve things that might need to be broadcast over and over again: an important speech, for example.

Arthur Askey pictured in Studio TC3 ahead of the *First Night* production, 29 June 1960.

Television presented a similar challenge. One of the best ways to record television was to film it, either by running film cameras alongside television cameras or by simply filming a television set as the broadcast was underway, a process known as telerecording. This was of archival benefit only, and the search was on for a medium that could almost instantaneously replay the images on screen. In the early 1950s BBC technicians developed VERA, the Vision Electronic Recording Apparatus, one of the first video recording machines. VERA was a room-sized apparatus that produced a grainy, degraded picture image thanks to the use of magnetic tape being run incredibly fast over a recording head – the same principle as audio tape. By the end of the decade, however, the BBC had switched over to the commercial product offered by Ampex, the American audio company. This off-the-shelf solution was used by broadcasters around the world, but the VERA project showed the levels of ingenuity and technical innovation required in the early days of the medium, especially the work of the BBC Research Department in Nightingale Square, in Balham, South London.

By the time Television Centre opened, Ampex's Quadruplex system was a global standard, albeit an expensive one. A single tape, capable of holding around 15 minutes of video, was $300, and the recording machine itself – the size of a catering oven – cost about $45,000. It was vastly better than the unwieldy and impractical VERA, which took up a whole room. Yet the switch to commercial video wasn't without major flaws – albeit economic ones, not technical. For a start, video technology was reusable; a tape could simply be overwritten with new information. Technicians and managers welcomed the innovation, but for archivists, it was disastrous. The BBC used Ampex 2" systems, as well as RCA video recorders, and budgets were always tight. Reusing tapes was commonplace. Yet as well as the raw financial implications, these losses reflected the ongoing transition from theatre culture; many shows were still performed live, and to preserve and rebroadcast that performance would effectively mean paying actors twice. Ultimately all these issues were addressed, but at the time it's safe to say the public didn't notice. It was a golden era for the medium, back when television's cultural importance was dominant, unrivalled and unprecedented. If it hadn't been on television, it hadn't happened. But there was no expectation of seeing things again.

Studio Control Room, 1960.
A suite such as this would have been operated by a sound mixer, presentation assistant/vision mixer, clerk, assistant senior television engineer and vision control engineer.

Above: the BBC staff canteen photographed in June 1960. During its peak, the restaurant had to cater for up to 6,000 employees.

Left: the BBC Club, on the upper floors of the Helios building, was a more exclusive venue than the canteen, reserved only for the highest-ranking members of management.

A self-contained city

Television Centre had its own unique culture. Many served out their entire careers within the complex, whether they worked in technical services, catering, programming or any one of hundreds of other jobs required to keep the building running. One BBC employee who worked in several key sectors of the building was Michael Eaton, who began his BBC career back in 1977. Eaton worked first in Audience Research at Langham Place (now the Langham Hotel) and then at the expansive Broadcasting House gramophone library, which contained in excess of 1.5 million items. From 1982, he was a Studio Supervisor at Broadcasting House, an essential element in programme making, responsible for managing the live studio audiences that would turn up for recordings and live broadcasts – "getting them in and out in one piece". Eaton ultimately moved into premises management, a job that would give him total behind-the-scenes access to Television Centre. "A lot of the way the BBC worked was very closely linked to the theatre," he recalls. "You had green rooms, front of house, stage managers, etc. Television Centre was at the top of the league table of buildings, and then within it there was a league table of areas. I was in charge of the Spur, where TV news was located. Clever, but highly strung people."

According to Eaton, there could be a "hard edge" to Television Centre, which became known as 'fortress BBC' due to the site's closed-off nature. The news team had come in from Alexandra Palace in 1969, long after other departments had moved to Television Centre, to occupy the section known as the Spur, the first part of the question mark-shaped floor plan to be added after the central circular building. The news staff had a traditional journalistic ethos, while in stark contrast the drama department exuded a more 'artistic' temperament. Somewhere in the middle, and answerable to no-one but themselves, were the Scenic Services department, occupying the first part of the complex and what eventually became known as the Scenery Block. "'Scene boys' were the heavy gang. Proper, tough London boys," says Eaton. "They were a rogues' gallery. They were also the powerhouse of the union. You didn't do anything to upset them. Scene boys could bring the show to a halt. They were hard grafters and they knew what they were doing."

Behind the camera, Television Centre had to function like a small city in order to keep its 6,000-strong workforce fed and watered. As well as the legendary canteen, it was home to the BBC Club, the main bar and the Helios bar, the latter intended for card-carrying members only, no guests. There was a strict hierarchy within the building, one that not only reflected the complex strata of BBC culture, but also the culture and different strata of society itself. From the brown-coated porters to the LRAs – Ladies' Room Attendants – and the many levels of producers, reporters, technicians and operators, the building was constantly busy, not to mention the visits from many hundreds of members of the public who came – often uninvited – to fill the streets of W12, depending on who was on the air.

Right: BBC Television Controllers, 1965. From left to right: David Attenborough, Michael Peacock, Huw Wheldon and Kenneth Adam.

Opposite page, top: British rock band The Who photographed in the Helios courtyard, 1966. From left to right: Keith Moon, John Entwistle, Pete Townshend, Roger Daltrey.

Opposite page, bottom left: football commentator Kenneth Wolstenholme celebrates the 1966 World Cup.

Opposite page, bottom right: Sonny and Cher photographed before performing on Top of the Pops, 1965.

The catering arrangements were a microcosm of this structure-loving organisation. The waitress-service canteen was joined by two cafeterias and a separate tea bar for each of the colour-coded studio areas. "You were well looked after here," says Eaton. "The whole idea was to keep people on site, not to go off to other restaurants or pubs, so that all that creativity stayed flowing around the corridors of Television Centre. It was a melting pot." From the democratic queue in the main canteen, where DJs would mingle with carpenters and newsreaders, to the sixth floor with its own suite for private dinners, served by a handy wine cellar on the fifth floor. This floor was the management zone, home to the 'gods of television' who over the years included Huw Wheldon, Bill Cotton, Paul Fox, Michael Grade and David Attenborough, who went on to become Director of Television from 1969 to 1973. Crucial decisions were made behind closed doors, while outside you heard the clatter and clink of drinks trolleys around the long circular corridor. Other services within Television Centre included a hairdresser (quite separate to the many make-up departments) and a travel agent, as well as a branch of national newsagent WH Smith and a florist.

There was a remarkable diversity of programming being made. As well as drama serials and plays, there were news and current affairs programmes – including coverage of every British general election from 1964 to 2010 – plus quiz games, chat shows, light entertainment spectaculars, sitcoms and one-offs. Throughout the 60s, 70s and 80s, Television Centre took over from Broadcasting House as the iconic symbol of the BBC. The front façade became the backdrop to the start of the annual Children in Need telethon in 1980. Shows with audiences in the tens of millions were made here, from big light-entertainment audience shows to sitcoms, ranging from *Fawlty Towers* to *Only Fools and Horses* (whose writer, John Sullivan, had begun his career at Television Centre's props department), to the more recent *Miranda*. It was also home to *Blue Peter,* the UK's most beloved children's programme and, perhaps most evocative of all, the chat show hosted by Michael Parkinson in two stints on the BBC between 1971 and 2004. "For decades, you can honestly say that the most famous, well-known people on the planet walked through Television Centre's reception area on their way to the Parkinson studio," says Michael Eaton. Over 2,000 guests in all were flown in from around the world to attend this weekly event, adding an impossible lustre to W12 as they wore down the terrazzo in front of the main reception desk, overlooked by a striking abstract mural by the artist John Piper.

Opposite page: Yvonne Littlewood directed the Eurovision Song Contest in 1963, which was broadcast to the rest of Europe from Television Centre. A helicopter flown by head helicopter pilot at BEA (now British Airways) circled the building to capture aerial footage to show off the new building.

Below: British artist John Piper working on his mural.

Bottom: the main lobby, or 'Stage Door' as it became known, with Piper's finished mural on the far wall.

Wood Lane, London W12 8QT. It's hard to overestimate the power of this London address, one that was read out or put up on screen during countless television programmes. Yet the building itself was more than an abstract postal address, however important that was in the era before digital communications. Although Television Centre is not a building that defines the skyline, the vast majority of people in the UK became more and more familiar with its form, not through visiting it in person or glimpsing it at a distance, but through seeing it regularly on their television screens.

Television Centre played countless bit parts in the Corporation's output, serving as backdrop, general location or even integral character. Shows like *Monty Python's Flying Circus, French & Saunders, Multi-Coloured Swap Shop* and many more used the location, including the distinctive curved façade, to place viewers firmly in the Corporation's heartland.

Meanwhile, new building work continued around the site throughout its life. As already mentioned, the Spur building, finished in 1969, completed the descender of the question mark, and became the headquarters of BBC News, with both offices and Studio 8. In 1978, the Blue Peter Garden was created, designed by the legendary Percy Thrower, but other new studios were added right up until 1998.

The end of Television Centre seemed swift, but the transition from broadcasting powerhouse to a new living and working destination – open to the public for the first time – was long and complex. As soon as the BBC's day-to-day operations left the site on 31 March 2013, Michael Eaton took on the role of overseeing the huge logistical process of packing up. "Everything had to be done the right way," he recalls, "from emptying tanks to tying off cables to making sure that licence payers' money wasn't seen to be wasted." It was a two-year process, during which time the bones of the building were stripped bare, including the thousands of miles of cabling laid down over more than fifty years of technological innovation.

The retained elements of the building perhaps represent the purist expressions of Graham Dawbarn's original, with two wings opening out either side of the curved façade: to the right, offices and retail, while to the left, the new, refurbished independent studio complex.

Now, as then, Television Centre is a building freighted with atmosphere, laden with memories. Towards the end of its working life, it was self-referentially used as a backdrop to dramas about the BBC itself, exploiting the different patina and details that survived from 1960 to the present day. In truth, from some angles, Television Centre gave off the impression of a fortress, a bulwark that shielded the creativity and culture within from the general public, but this was also part of television's magic. The medium introduced us to a new world of artifice and transience, faked spaces and wholly invented scenarios that became visual shorthand for how we perceive the world – the newsreader, the weather presenter, the game show, the sitcom. For those not in the industry, it almost comes as a surprise to discover physical spaces behind this thin façade, the whole cities of industry that support these ephemeral moments. Dawbarn himself wrote that a building of this significance "should avoid on the one hand a pompous heaviness and on the other... too much ephemeral fancy and self-conscious trickery". In many respects, technological change doomed the architectural form of Television Centre from the outset. But the building absorbed half a century of alterations, not just in broadcasting technology itself but in the duration, ambition and sophistication of the programming. Television Centre has remained an enduring symbol during changing times.

From Westway
to Westfield

The 1960s were a time of shining optimism but also extraordinary destruction. All over the country, bold plans for the reconstruction of urban centres and the creation of new roads saw change on an unprecedented scale. By the time the first stage of Television Centre was completed in 1960, plans for the transformation of London's transport routes were well-advanced. Television Centre occupied just a small part of the original White City site, and by the time of its construction the northernmost part of the postcode was effectively hemmed in by the upgraded A40, a main arterial road out of London. Its official name, the London to Fishguard Trunk Road, signals its scope, reaching all the way from the City of London to the west coast of Wales, 262 miles away. White City originally stood on the scrubby suburbs on the edge of the city. The boundaries of the Great Western Road to the north and the Uxbridge Road to the south were major thoroughfares, leading to the Middlesex parishes of Hillingdon, Cowley and Uxbridge, but not yet the broad tarmac barriers they became.

These small towns and villages were soon part of London's sprawl for, like so much of modern London, W12 was shaped by transportation – first railways, then cars and then finally aircraft. As the car rose to pre-eminence in the post-war era, unshackled by rationing and export restrictions, town planners sought ever more intrusive ways of shoehorning the automobile into the city. The wild open spaces of Wormwood Scrubs were tempered by the arrival of the eponymous prison and Hammersmith Hospital, while the land to the east of White City was shaped by the massive rail depot, sidings, storage and power station created to serve the Central Line. Further east of that, acting as a barrier to the elegant crescents, mansions and gardens of Holland Park, Kensington and Notting Hill, is the A3220, a dual carriageway formerly known as the M41 – just half a mile long.

This road is one of the surviving remnants of Ringway 1, the grandiose scheme to bring an elevated orbital motorway to inner London. The Ringways plan was the epitome of 1960s planning, evolving out of the 1943 County of London Plan and the Greater London Plan of 1944, both overseen by Patrick Abercrombie. Abercrombie saw opportunity in the destruction caused during the war and proposed a series of circular routes around London to bring the motorist into the heart of the city. The wholesale demolition required by his suggested innermost ring, 'A', was too much during a time of austerity and the idea was shelved, but the principles were revised in the mid-1960s with the Ringways scheme. No less destructive, Ringway 1 roughly aligned with Abercrombie's Ring B, an elevated concrete ribbon that inevitably sliced through some of the oldest and most interesting parts of historic London. Along with the stubby section of the A3220, the only other built section was the Westway, which fulfilled its futuristic remit, only to be cruelly truncated at the West Cross Route Junction, an elevated roundabout with unfinished spurs that jut out towards Victorian terraces.

Left: the West Cross Route junction under construction, late 1960s. This elevated roundabout is the meeting point of the West Cross Route (A3220) and the Westway (A40). Unfinished spurs, visible on the right of the roundabout, still exist to this day, and would have carried the A3220 further north as part of Patrick Abercrombie's grand Ringway 1 plan. White City Stadium can be seen in the top left.

Right: a housing protest, 1970, sees residents unfurling a large banner next to the Westway.

Below right: a map of the Ringway roads as proposed in the 1943 County of London Plan.

Bottom: Patrick Abercrombie (1879–1957), architect and town planner. Following the Second World War, Abercrombie was influential in the large-scale rebuilding of London. He created the County of London Plan and the Greater London Plan.

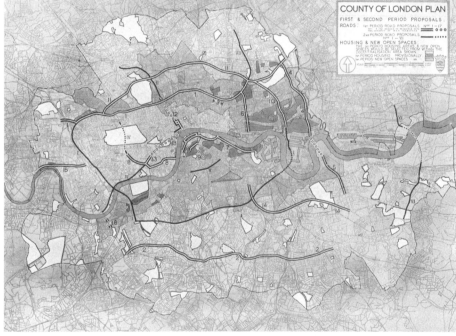

The elevated A40 dual carriageway, also known as the Westway, winding through Ladbroke Grove, 1975. The road was opened as the A40(M) in 1970 and carries traffic above London for 3.5 miles, from Marylebone to White City.

Thankfully, attitudes and intentions shifted and the eventual abandonment of the Ringways scheme in the 1970s left W12 largely intact. For a time, the White City of the British Broadcasting Corporation continued to co-exist with the White City of decades past. The stadium itself was a venerable survivor, although athletics and football gave way to speedway and greyhound racing. The structure managed to survive all the way into the mid-80s, with a half-century of dog racing coming to an end on 22 September 1984. By early 1985, the entire stadium had been demolished. It was the end of an era, as well as the passing of a building that had pioneered the idea of a modern multi-sports stadium.

The site was redeveloped by the BBC, starting with Scott Brownrigg & Turner's White City One in 1990. The new home for the Corporation's current affairs and educational programming, White City One lacked the attention to design detail that defined Broadcasting House and Television Centre. The site was continually expanded, and by 2004 it had become Media Village, with dedicated buildings for broadcasting and BBC Worldwide, the commercial arm of the Corporation. Plans for a spectacular new concert hall that was also a rehearsal space for the BBC's three orchestras were drawn up by Foreign Office Architects. The ribbon-like structure was never realised.

The quasi-industrial appearance of the BBC's Media Village facility was very much in keeping with the late-century character of White City. Low-rise warehouses co-existed with railway sidings and sheds, both struggling to see over the elevated concrete ramps of the Westway, while quirky in-fill businesses like riding stables filled the gaps between the wholesalers, garages and storage centres. During the Second World War, parts of the White City exhibition ground had been given over to small-scale manufacture, including aviation, with the London Aircraft Production (LAP) Group established to build the Handley Page Halifax bomber occupying some of the surviving exhibition buildings. Today, history is left only in the street names – South Africa Road, Canada Way, Australia Road.

Bit by bit, light industry has given way to a new emphasis on retail, residential and educational space – with Television Centre as a catalyst for the area's regeneration. The low-rise warehousing has been replaced by new apartment blocks, offices and university research centres. Former BBC buildings east of Wood Lane and north of the A40 were sold to Imperial College in 2009 and the site is currently being redeveloped as the institution's White City Campus, which includes the Michael Uren Biomedical Engineering Research Hub by Allies and Morrison, and a 35-storey residential tower by PLP Architects. Imperial's campus extends to both sides of the A40, with the new Invention Rooms community shared space as the first part of a long-term extension to the south of the site.

Other focal points include White City Living by Berkeley St James, 1,800 new homes directly adjacent to Television Centre. The development even makes a deliberate reference to the shimmering palaces of the Franco-British Exhibition, by using white concrete panelling as a primary cladding material. The current landscape of W12 is looking dramatically different.

AT THE
WHITE CITY

BOOK TO
WOOD LANE
TUBE STATION

The most radical change in the area was the coming of Westfield London. Back in 1997, initial plans for a vast new commercial complex above the Central Line White City depot were proposed by Chelsfield plc. The huge brownfield redevelopment project began in 2003 and was taken over by the Australian developers Westfield the following year. After four years of construction, involving some 8,000 contractors, Westfield London opened in October 2008, containing some 150,000 square metres of retail space. The site was expanded yet again in 2018, creating Europe's largest shopping centre. For many, Westfield defines the future of retail, a carefully maintained environment where the myriad brands and retailers can co-exist, delivering a self-contained shopping, dining and entertainment experience.

This desire for a more experiential environment also drove the evolution of the rest of the area. By 2015, Media Village had become White City Place with the decanting of BBC departments to Salford, Broadcasting House and elsewhere in the Corporation's property empire. The new development repurposed and refurbished the existing BBC buildings to make dedicated space for small creative businesses in the renamed MediaWorks, WestWorks and Garden House. The latter is a new facility for the Royal College of Art and will eventually house programmes from both the School of Communication and School of Architecture. White City Place also contains new places to eat and drink, set alongside a re-landscaped Central Avenue.

In its new guise, White City is an assemblage of major developments, each created in concert with one another and mindful of the views, light and connections between them. The surrounding landscape has been unified and architecture co-ordinated, but each development has an identity that remains distinct. Westfield has now been a fixture for a decade, with adjoining residential projects like White City Living enhancing the residential atmosphere of an area that was once dominated by light industry, with scarcely an apartment or house in sight.

In February 2013, just before the BBC moved out of Television Centre, Google was invited to send its mapping systems into the building to create a virtual archive of the warren of offices and studio spaces. Clicking around them today it is hard to feel anything but nostalgia, with modern technology acting as a filter through which the workaday offices and communal spaces become a mythological place, resonating with the memories of the people and programmes that defined it to the world. Today, W12 has been reborn as a new destination, an important component of a more adventurous, self-confident London that embraces the many complexities and interwoven histories that shape the modern city. At the heart of the postcode is Television Centre, a focal point for transformation and radical redevelopment that still retains a valuable sense of the past.

An aerial photograph from early 2018 shows the scale of the transformation happening in White City today, with Television Centre at the heart of the area.

2013: the BBC moves out

Technology

Radio

Business Daily

Weekend Programmes

Interactive

BBC World

JOURNALISM
PORTAL
HELP
Call ext: 57134

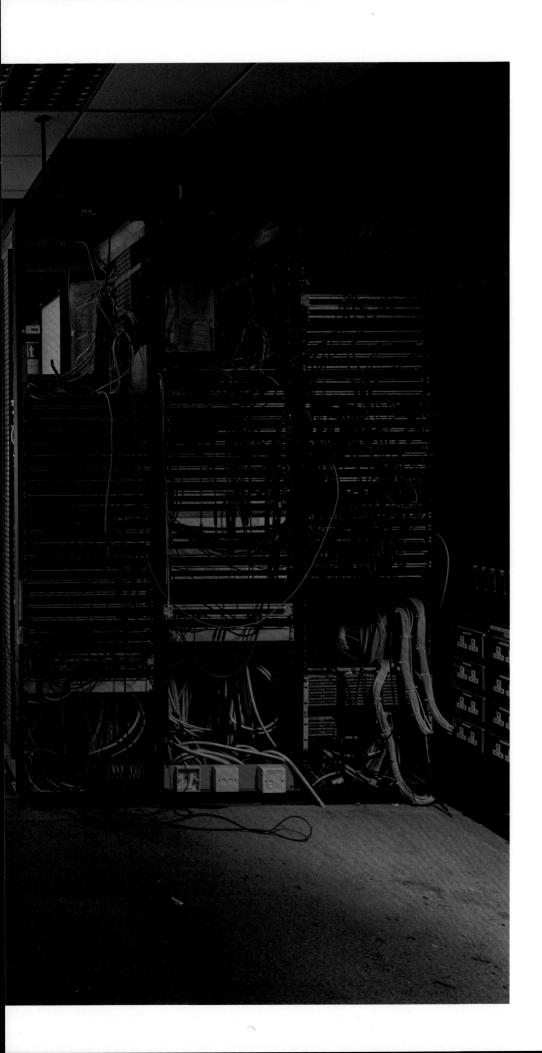

Television Centre reimagined

The end of the BBC era was bittersweet, but the knowledge that Television Centre would be reborn with a new purpose, set amidst a far more open and welcoming environment and new public spaces, tempered the sadness at leaving the site that had been so integral to the Corporation's history and ethos. Once stripped of its many internal strata of technology – like layers of geological sediment going back through time to reveal the evolution of the industry – the building didn't stay empty for long. Stanhope, with its development partners Mitsui Fudosan and Alberta Investment Management Company, acquired the site on 20 July 2012.

White City still retains its close connection to the BBC, not only because of BBC Studios (which includes the Corporation's commercial arm formerly known as BBC Worldwide), but also thanks to the many innovation and technical support services in the area, as well as new businesses associated with media and broadcasting that have arrived to bolster the area's distinct creative character. From the outset, the intention was to retain and build on this character, supplementing it with the retention of three refurbished television studios. In the long term, there is also the ongoing expansion of Imperial College's campus to the north, the arrival of major commercial clients like The White Company and Publicis Media – which has six UK creative agencies at White City – and the opening of a new outpost of the media-centric Soho House members' club and hotel, along with restaurants including Patty & Bun, Kricket, Homeslice and Bluebird Café.

Creating a thriving new city district is the ultimate goal of every planner and architect. London's eclectic mix of history, heritage, cultures, uses, ambitions and expectations adds a layer of uncertainty to almost every decision about large-scale development. Stanhope approached the Television Centre site with very clear intentions about the enduring identity and ongoing associations of this historic complex. From the earliest discussions with the BBC, which was only too mindful of the intense affection for the buildings, the idea was to develop a mixed-use development, with a masterplan drawn up by an accomplished firm of architects. Allford Hall Monaghan Morris have overseen the project, from the initial discussions through to the planning consultation, application and finally the construction itself. Founded by Simon Allford, Jonathan Hall, Paul Monaghan and Peter Morris in 1989, AHMM has won numerous awards, including the prestigious RIBA Stirling Prize in 2015.

AHMM's contemporary approach was deeply sympathetic to the original architecture of Television Centre. The studio's work is a modern interpretation of the fundamental tenets of modernism – clean lines, contemporary materials and technologies, the occasional highlight of colour and form and, above all, a commitment to an intelligent, pragmatic but always warm and human functionalism.

Paul Monaghan, founder and director of Allford Hall Monaghan Morris (AHMM).

Paul Monaghan, the partner in charge of the project, describes AHMM's approach as one of quiet, respectful enhancement. "One of our very first sketches ended up being the scheme we built," he says, recalling the early days of design development back in 2011 and inadvertently drawing a parallel with Graham Dawbarn's quasi-mythological 'back of an envelope' sketch. "One of our touchstones for the project was that you shouldn't be able to tell that we've been here," Monaghan continues. "Although the new office wing is slightly like the building it replaces, it looks as if it has always been there. You can't really see what's new and what's old."

The following pages highlight some of the themes that ran throughout AHMM's approach.

Primary moves

The unique 'question mark' masterplan for the Television Centre site was conceived – literally on the back of an envelope – by the BBC's architect Graham Dawbarn in 1949. The new buildings would together create the world's largest and most sophisticated 'factory for television'.

Over the years the Television Centre buildings were repeatedly adapted to respond to the rapid growth of television and its associated technologies, with new additions, extensions and refurbishments undertaken. However, the masterplan remained remarkably untouched. And it still establishes the diagram for the site, the new masterplan respecting Dawbarn's original design intent by setting up a series of concentric elements which radiate outwards from the central Helios Plaza, which continues to be at the heart of the neighbourhood.

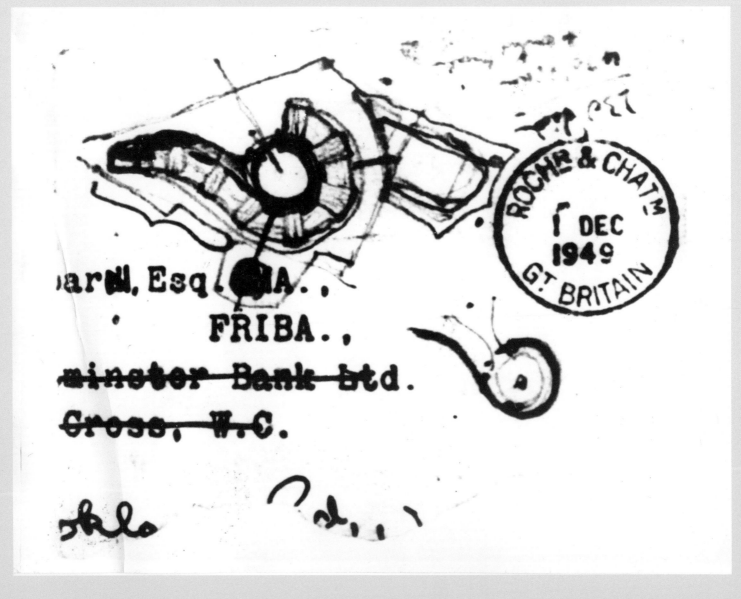

Opposite page: Graham Dawbarn's earliest sketch for the Television Centre complex, drawn on the back of an envelope in 1949. The iconic 'question mark' design has never been lost.

Right: a scale model of AHMM's masterplan for the site. The circular Helios building has been retained, along with Studios 1, 2 and 3, which radiate outwards from the central ring. The surrounding block which once housed Studios 4 to 7 has been replaced by the Crescent, an all-new building that wraps around the Helios, creating a new curved garden between the two structures.

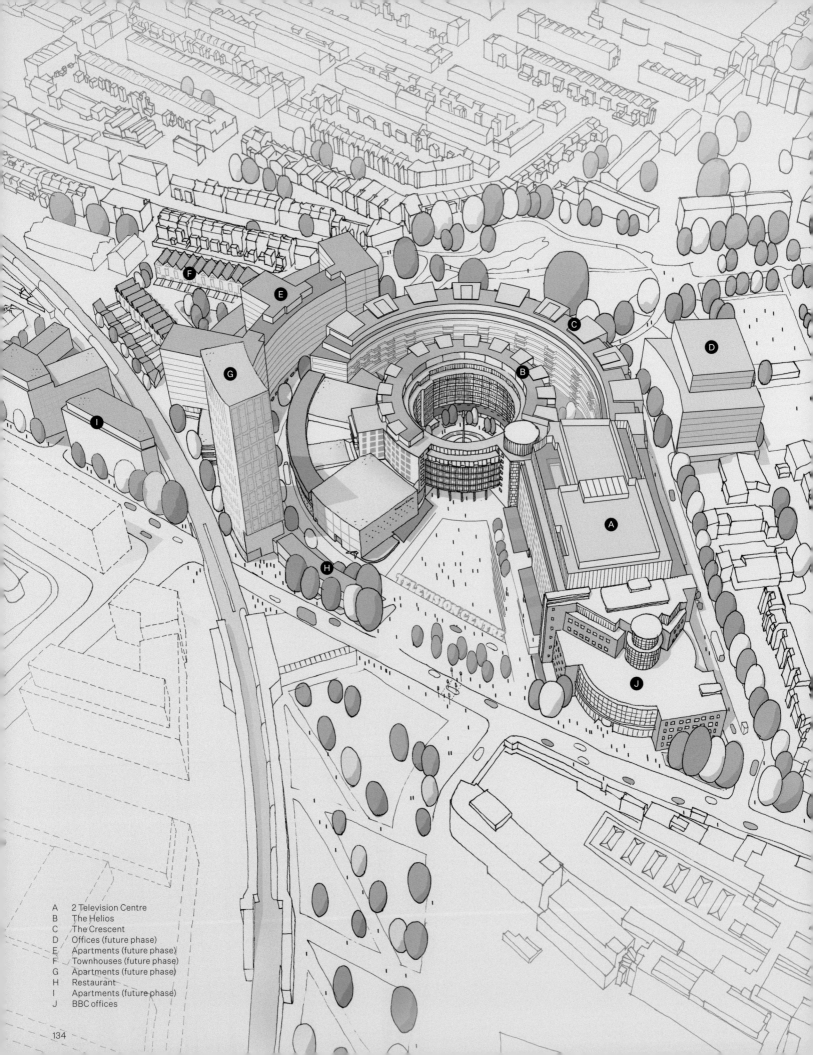

A   2 Television Centre
B   The Helios
C   The Crescent
D   Offices (future phase)
E   Apartments (future phase)
F   Townhouses (future phase)
G   Apartments (future phase)
H   Restaurant
I   Apartments (future phase)
J   BBC offices

Extraordinary mix

The original 'television factory' felt like a small city because so many activities were brought together on one site: studios, offices, workshops and leisure. Similarly, the new masterplan brings together an unusually rich mixture of uses to enable a new community to live, work and play at White City.

The BBC continues to have a presence on site, with Studios 1, 2 and 3 at the inner curve of the question mark and the BBC Studios offices at its tip on Wood Lane. 2 Television Centre, in the stem of the question mark, is a new, nine-storey office hub for creative industries, with more office space sitting on the park edge of the site, where the restaurant block once stood.

Elsewhere, the concentric rings of the masterplan are made up of around 950 new homes, often with retail at the lower levels. A hotel, gym, members' club, cinema and pool complete the mix of uses.

Living landscape

While the famous Television Centre forecourt and Helios Courtyard were a familiar backdrop to many BBC viewers, they were off-limits to all but BBC employees, talent and guests. The masterplan opens the site to the public for the first time, stitching the site back into the surrounding communities and giving access into Hammersmith Park. The forecourt and courtyard link to a series of private gardens and green courtyards which reinforce the concentric rings of the masterplan.

The forecourt, facing onto Wood Lane and surrounded by cafés, restaurants and a south-facing terrace, has been reinvented as a space for a variety of community activities. An open, flexible stage area can host screenings, music performances and food markets, while denser woodland planting and park-like areas for play give a softer setting to the main buildings. The Helios Courtyard remains the hub of the masterplan, with the statue of Helios at its centre set in fountains and new planting.

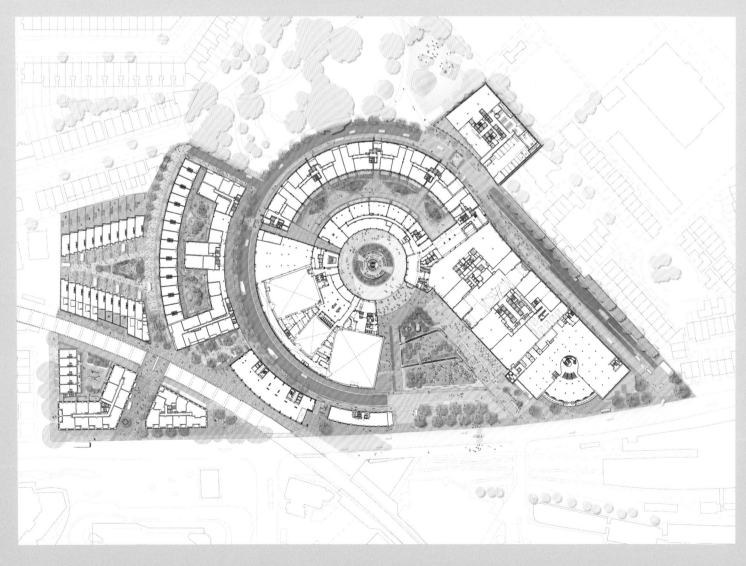

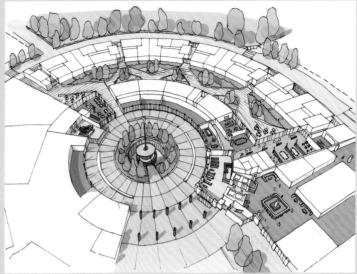

Opposite page: a plan of the
landscaping that surrounds the
Television Centre site, designed
by Gillespies.

Above: some of AHMM's early
sketches show the integration of
greenery throughout the scheme.

Left: a 1:100 scale model of the Helios courtyard. The façade is Grade II listed; accordingly the original mosaic patterns and Crittal windows have been carefully restored.

The spirit of Television Centre

While the BBC has a scaled-back working presence at Television Centre, the Corporation's identity, and its accompanying values of creativity and innovation, continue to be manifest across the scheme. Moving through the site, views familiar to millions of viewers at home have been preserved, and it is difficult to see where new and old begin and end.

The heritage significance of the complex is evident in its Grade II listing, which covers the forecourt and studio façade, Studio 1, the interior of the original stage door, and the Helios Courtyard. The buildings retain many examples of original mid-century modern design in their materials and artwork, most notably the John Piper mosaic at the stage door, which is now a lobby for residents. These important indicators of the building's past have either been preserved – in the case of the artworks, slab-serif signage and original ceramic mosaics – or reinterpreted in the fit-out and finishes of apartments and offices as bespoke tiling and Italian terrazzo surfaces.

The building's heritage is also celebrated in colour. When completed in 1960, the cladding to the forecourt façade was in two shades of blue, but an original 1956 watercolour shows that this cladding was intended to be red. When restoring the façade of the 'drum' the original intended colour was reinstated – and further referenced in the red tones used in the interiors and elsewhere in the development.

Above: a 1:25 scale 'doll's house' model of a one-bedroom apartment within the historic inner Helios. These spaces were formerly BBC production offices.

Right: this original watercolour painting by Frank A. Weemys, dated March 1956, was uncovered in the BBC's art collection. It inspired the decision to return the outward-facing façade of the Helios to its original red colour.

A place to live...

For the first time, Television Centre has become a place to live, a new community evolving out of the site's varied mix of uses and shared indoor and outdoor spaces.

A doughnut-shaped block of around 160 residential apartments and a small hotel – named the Helios – follows the footprint of the original drum of TV executives' offices at the centre of the site. The courtyard in the middle has been opened up and landscaped to give access to a below-ground gym, and the gilded Helios statue by TB Huxley-Jones returned. The fountains at the base of its obelisk have been restored along with sculptures representing sound and vision.

The Crescent, a new-build development of 270 apartments, wraps around the Helios, replicating the curve of the original drum. The top two floors of the eight-storey block step back, breaking up the roofline. All apartments have views down into a green courtyard, out across Hammersmith Park, or both.

Left: sketches by AHMM show the consideration given to the interior palette for the scheme, which celebrates the mid-century design and materials of the original building. These examples went on to inform the look of the restored Helios lobby and residents' lounge.

Left: a 1:25 scale model of a Crescent apartment.

Below: a 1:100 scale model of the building's façade, which connects with neighbouring Hammersmith Park and provides generous balconies to all apartments overlooking the green space.

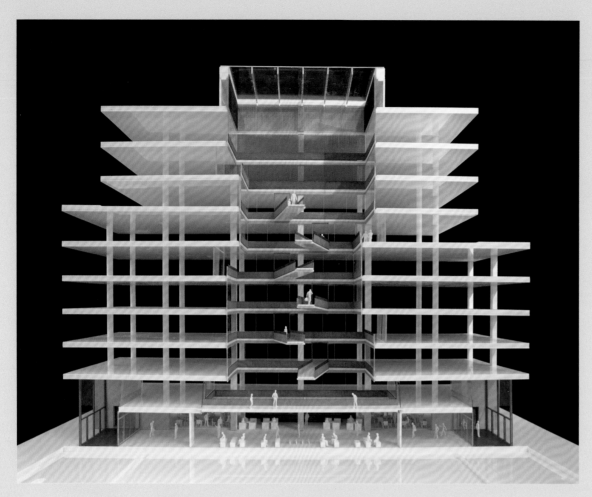

This page, top and below right: a model and cutaway sketch of the 2 Television Centre atrium show the bridges which cross the space dramatically on each floor.

Below left: the red stair that winds up through the building references the original red façade of the Helios.

Opposite page: a sketch of the 'inner street' – a public thoroughfare that runs across the building beneath the atrium, connecting the public forecourt to the outer road, Wood Crescent. Restaurants and cafés flank the space at either end.

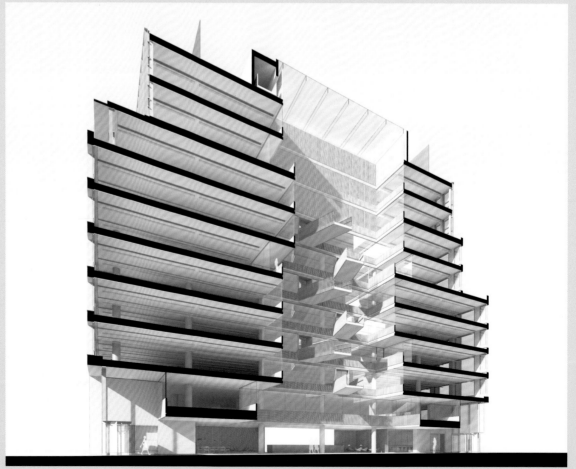

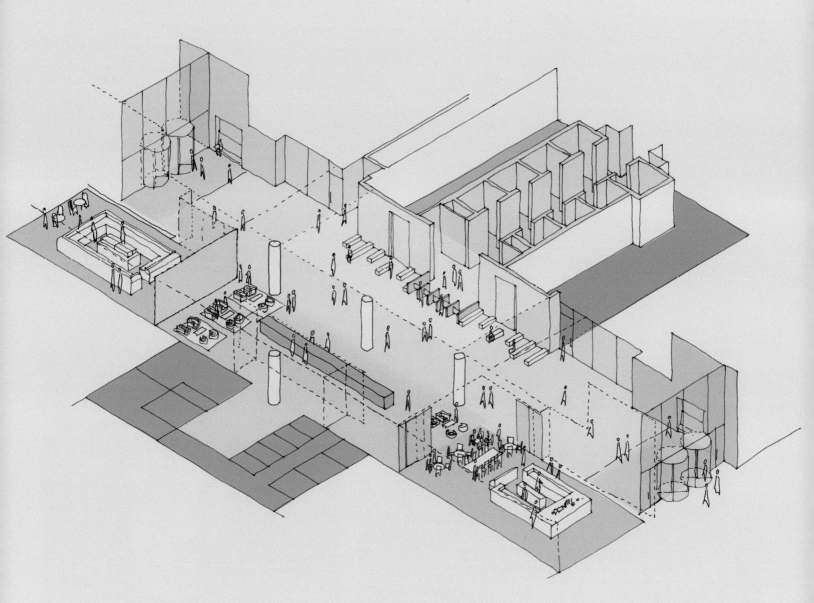

...and a place to work

Television Centre also continues to be a place to work. The BBC still makes programmes in the refurbished Studios 1, 2 and 3, which enclose the south-eastern side of the Helios plaza. Here, the back-of-house areas have been renewed so the studios can operate independently, and the interiors stripped back to their brick and concrete structure. The BBC's heritage is evident in artworks based on the iconic test card graphic, and 'on air' lightboxes.

In contrast, 2 Television Centre is a brand-new place of work. The building functions more like a village of small offices rather than a single headquarters, and has become the new home of Publicis Media and The White Company. The internal spaces open onto a central street, open to the public as a connection through the site, with a dramatically bridged atrium above.

Design showcase

The masterplan covers a wide range of typologies and contexts, from dwellings set in the raw spaces of the original, historic building fabric, to new stand-alone family homes in the southern neighbourhood. As a result, it presents a great shopfront for British design.

To demonstrate the many different design approaches possible in a development of this scale, a talented cohort of architectural practices have collaborated across the site, both up-and-coming studios and more well-established firms. Morris + Company, dRMM, Mikhail Riches and MaccreanorLavington have each designed a plot within the masterplan, while Coffey Architects, Haptic, Piercy&Company and Archer Humphryes each created a series of apartment interiors within the Helios and Crescent buildings.

Opposite page: some of the
additional buildings that will
form the second phase of
Television Centre's masterplan.
Clockwise from top left: Plot
F by Mikhail Riches; Plot H by
MaccreanorLavington; Plot F;
Plot D by Morris+Company.

Above: portraits of some of the
British practices who were invited
by AHMM to design apartment
interiors for the Helios and
Crescent. Clockwise from top left:
Haptic, Piercy&Company, Archer
Humphryes, Coffey Architects.

In many respects, AHMM represents the continuation of a distinguished design lineage that began with the purist functionalism of the pre-war Modernists and gradually evolved through the absorption of Scandinavian and other regional influences in the 1950s and 60s, becoming a fully formed expression of British attitudes to design and technology and the role of architecture in defining community and society. Monaghan speaks of making a modest, rather than an overwhelming design statement – "we are the bridesmaids, not the bride" – and points out how AHMM's plan subtly enhances and refocuses the attention on the best bits of the original building. "The big change was replacing five of the studios with the residential block, but also keeping the big, sweeping curve," he explains. "We also tried to ensure that the interiors had the same attention to detail as the original building, from storage to tiling to materials." Television Centre was opened in 1960, at the start of a decade of intense change and development in both culture and technology. Although intended to evolve and change over time, the fundamental components of the design, namely the circular Helios building, with its inner ring courtyard, were typical of the ethos and aesthetics of the era.

It was therefore all the more important that these elements were retained, restored and brought to the forefront of the new Television Centre. The Television Centre building was designated Grade II in July 2009 on account of the historic interest of the BBC's role and the architectural and design quality of several key components, including the central ring structure, the original Studio 1, and decorative elements like TB Huxley-Jones' sculpture of Helios and the large mural by John Piper in the main reception area. The ad-hoc nature of the site – and of the evolution of the BBC itself – often resulted in compromising or contrasting additions to the site. AHMM's scheme subdivided the site into eight smaller plots, as well as making preliminary planning applications that allowed the BBC to retain an autonomous presence on part of the site, should major works occur. "Stanhope understand design and also that design and interiors are tied together," Monaghan says. "We also wanted a mix of uses so it wasn't just a dormitory. And it was important to preserve the big spaces – the studio wall with its signage, the Helios courtyard, the curved 'superlobby' that runs around the building."

These subdivisions signalled the immense complexity of the site as well as the challenges facing the architectural team. A total of 432 new residential units, including 162 arranged around the iconic form of the inner ring, had to be plotted and planned within a hugely complex structure, much of which required substantial reinforcement and enhancement to bring it up to modern residential standards. The end result is set within 14 acres of new landscaping, overseen by the London studio of Gillespies.

Inside, residents have access to a private lounge and screening room and a subterranean gymnasium with 17-metre swimming pool managed by Soho House. New restaurants and retail, a small hotel and a new three-screen independent Electric Cinema bring a vibrant quality of life to the site, enhanced too by the presence of three bustling cutting-edge television studios, utilising the refurbished original structures of the BBC's Studios 1, 2 and 3, making it once again the home of television light entertainment.

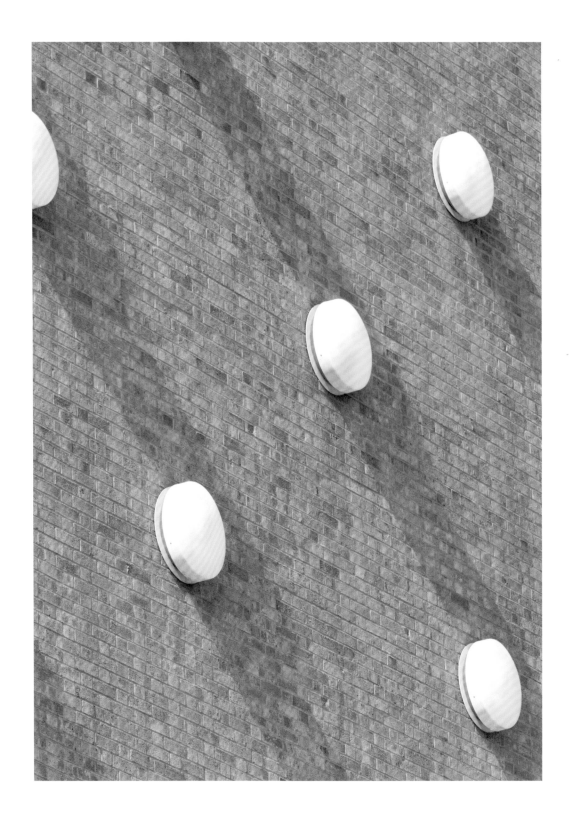

BBC Studios

"The BBC had to make sure that the legacy of their history was celebrated and preserved," says Alistair Shaw, MD of the project at Stanhope. "It wasn't just about the bid, but about choosing a developer they trusted. Our promise was that there would be a proper celebration of their legacy and the original use of the building going forward." Stanhope's approach was unique in that it offered to put the BBC at centre stage, as a true partner in the development.

The BBC's new facilities, known as BBC Studios, are a jewel in the crown of the Television Centre development. Fulfilling the Corporation's desire to preserve its heritage, while also fulfilling a commercial and cultural function, BBC Studios is a complex of three state-of-the-art studios and post-production facilities, using the footprints of the original broadcast studios that fanned out from the inner ring.

TC1, TC2 and TC3 provide a total of over 22,000 square feet of shooting space, with dedicated storage, backstage and crew areas, as well as scenery loading bays and audience handling areas. Compared to the original BBC Television Centre, there is now a wealth of options for entertainment and dining on the doorstep of the new facility. "All production companies want a studio as well as somewhere to work, to eat, to sleep, to chat," says Shaw. "These studios represent a new era of commercialisation for the BBC." Major terrestrial shows made there, like *The Jonathan Ross Show* (currently made for ITV) and *The Graham Norton Show*, have already made their mark on the studio complex, drawing a direct lineage back to the heyday of Parkinson et al., and the golden era of the original complex. Up to 600 audience members can be accommodated in the largest studio. "We wanted to make some big moves in the audience experience," says Shaw. "You used to be locked outside on Wood Lane for hours on end and then turfed out the minute filming had finished. Today, Television Centre offers a real day out."

The Helios
and Crescent

AHMM's plan christened the ring building the Helios, a crisply contemporary space that retains its mid-century origins, with terrazzo and polished concrete bringing light into the very heart of the complex. "That 1950s architecture is quite timeless," architect Paul Monaghan notes, pointing out that one major change – the shift from blue to red on the circular façade – has been handled so sensitively that many people can't even remember the original colour. On the upper levels are a series of penthouses and terraces, together with the rooftop location of the newest outpost of Soho House.

The Helios Apartments are joined by the Crescent, a new block that curves around the original BBC 'doughnut', emphasising its form and creating a new private courtyard within, with outward views across Hammersmith Park. The new gymnasium is located beneath the original circular courtyard, beneath the refurbished sculpture and reinstated fountain.

The courtyard is also adjoining the main reception, with its restored John Piper mural. Comprising many tens of thousands of coloured ceramic pieces, the mural was a commission from an artist with a strong sense of public service – Piper was an official war artist in the Second World War – and also an awareness of the potential and significance of television as a medium (before the war, he had presented some of the earliest arts programmes ever televised). The three-metre tall statue of Helios, the Greek god of the sun, was also removed temporarily for restoration, along with the two smaller sculptures representing sound and vision that sit at the fountain's base. PAYE Conservation, a specialist company with experience of working with over 2,000 years of architectural history, cleaned and re-gilded Huxley-Jones' mighty bronze figure, with real gold leaf rather than the gold paint used back in the early 1960s, possibly as a cost-cutting measure.

These spaces form the core of the revitalised Television Centre, as well as carrying the strongest weight of heritage and history. From the start of the project, AHMM's approach was guided by the need to preserve the best elements of Graham Dawbarn's original design. The key spaces were the main lobby, known for decades as the 'Stage Door' entrance to BBC Television Centre, and the South Hall space, together with the impressive endless loops of glazed corridors that shaped the spatial experience of the inner ring, linked by an impressively elegant modernist staircase rising up through an atrium with fluted walls, ribbon-thin metal balustrades and a winding wooden handrail.

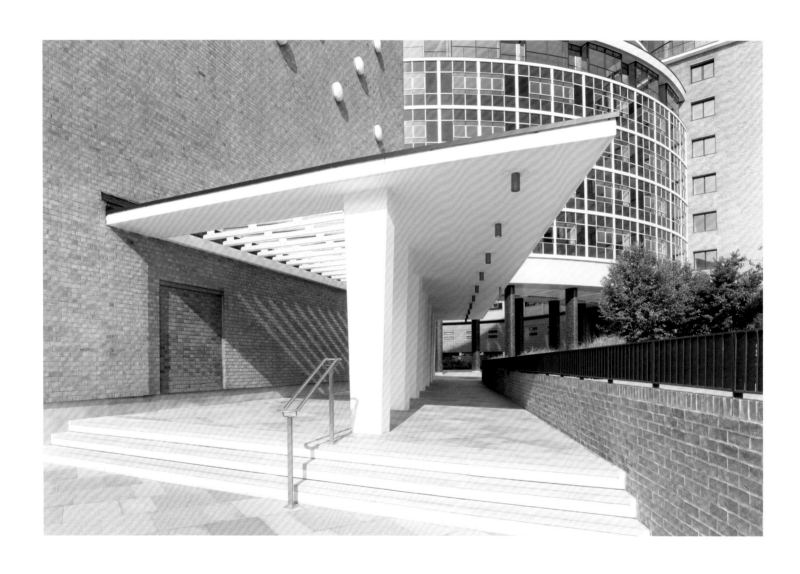

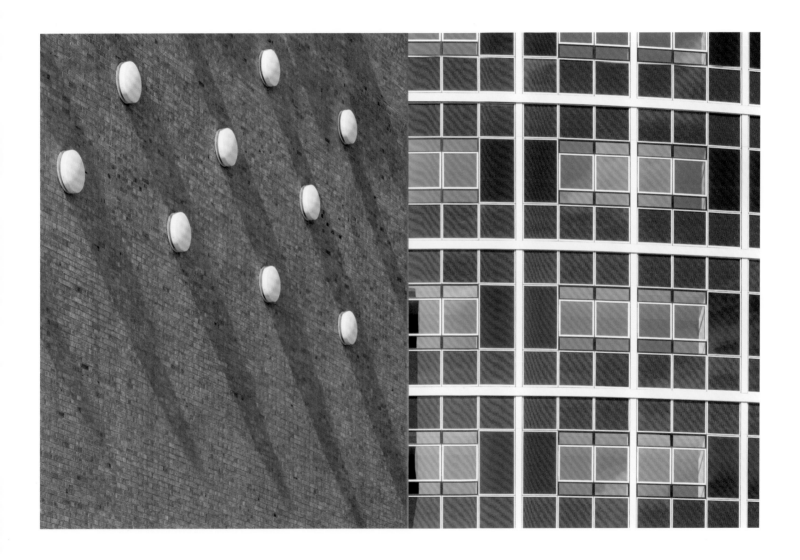

Below: the Helios apartments replace BBC production offices, encircling TB Huxley-Jones's statue at the centre of the courtyard. The interiors celebrate the original structure with exposed structural concrete ceilings and restored Crittal windows.

Opposite page: the mid-century-inspired interior palette features terrazzo, oak, and bespoke geometric tiles inspired by the work of American ceramicist Edith Heath.

Stripping away decades of additions meant that the newly christened Helios building effectively needed a new external façade at the rear, especially at ground level, where a new colonnade unites the generous residents' spaces with the new planting and landscaping, with the curve of the building creating ever-shifting perspectives. The Courtyard Apartments within the Helios epitomise the mid-century qualities of Dawbarn's building. Originally housing BBC production offices, the spaces have been transformed into a collection of airy modern apartments, making full use of the full-width Crittall glazing. The choice of materials and finishes was intended to evoke the heyday of the building and the BBC, combining terrazzo with concrete, ceramics and wood.

The Helios Apartments sit above a run of Garden Apartments and below the collection of Helios penthouses, while the adjoining Crescent Apartments are housed in a striking new building by AHMM. Generous balconies project out of the curving brick façade, with interiors furnished with a mix of modern pieces and heritage-inspired finishes. A series of geometric tile designs were especially created for the project, inspired by the work of Edith Heath, the acclaimed American ceramicist known for her mid-twentieth-century style forms.

Stanhope invited designers and neighbouring retailers to collaborate on a series of show apartments. The list includes cosy contemporary spaces by Suzy Hoodless, The White Company and West Elm. The John Lewis-styled apartment imagines an ultra-connected smart home, while fashion designer Bella Freud took a decidedly 70s-modern approach.

Above: the Crescent, viewed from Hammersmith Park. The all-new circular form follows the original footprint of the building, but apartments replace Studios 4 to 7. Whereas the BBC site was strictly off-limits to the public, the new masterplan connects with the park and creates a new pedestrian route through to Wood Lane.

Opposite page: interior details from the Crescent. All apartments either have a view into the curved residents' garden, out towards Hammersmith Park, or both.

The most extravagant expression of Television Centre's design ethos is represented in the new penthouses, arranged around the uppermost level of the Helios and the Crescent. "We made the roofscape more dramatic," explains Paul Monaghan of AHMM, "with a cascading series of terraces for the penthouses that gives a mansion block-like character."

With skyline views of London and generous terraces, these penthouses represent a truly bespoke approach to architecture and interiors, with a select group of invited architects transforming the spaces into a unique grouping of the very best of modern residential design. The firms involved include Piercy&Company, Coffey Architects, Haptic, AHMM and Archer Humphryes, while the fashion designer Bella Freud was also invited to oversee one of the interiors in collaboration with local firm Retrouvius. Yet although the penthouses are the apex of any large-scale development, the quality that flows down through Television Centre ensures that every apartment within the Helios and the Crescent features the same care and attention to design detail.

The view from the eighth floor, above the curved residents' garden which runs between the restored circular Helios building and the all-new Crescent. Penthouse apartments are arranged at this level.

In November 2014, photographer Lee Mawdsley was invited to document the Television Centre site following the BBC's departure. He spent two weeks exploring the grounds before the demolition and construction crews arrived.

In June 2018 he returned to White City to see the reimagined buildings. The following pages were shot as deliberate diptychs, comparing 'before' and 'after'. Some are literal; the same space transformed. Some are more poetic; a playful contrast of composition and form.

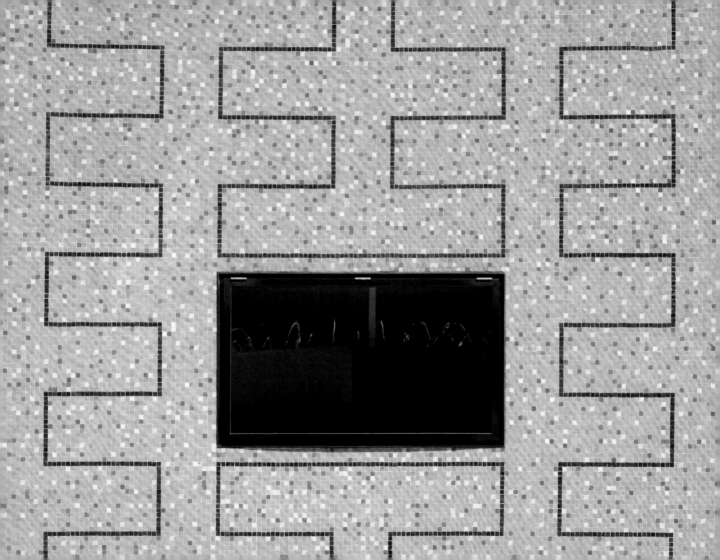

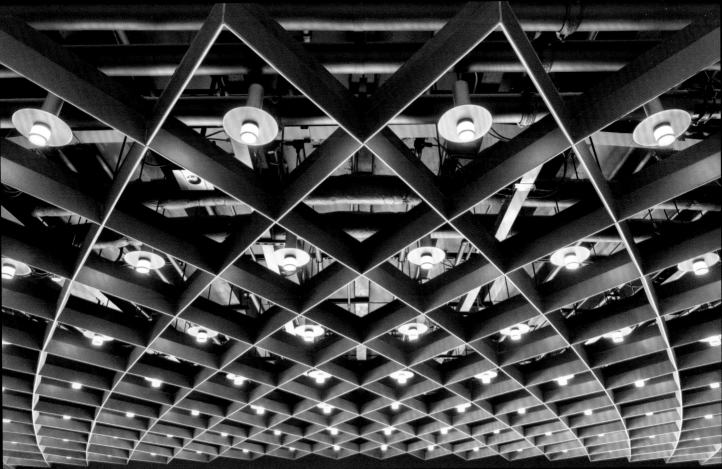

Consultation and collaboration

Stanhope's overall vision for the Television Centre site had to be fully formed right from the start of the planning process, thanks to the intensive research undertaken by AHMM, Gillespies and the other key stakeholders. But Television Centre is also part of a wider neighbourhood, White City, and an ongoing process of collaboration and consultation has knitted the development into its neighbourhood. White City was identified as one of the capital's many 'Opportunity Areas' in the Greater London Assembly's original 2004 London Plan. "This is very much an era of reaching out to other developers," says Stanhope's Alistair Shaw. "The success of Television Centre depended on others doing things very well, particularly in the public realm. We plan the spaces between the buildings very carefully, and we wanted this to ripple out."

There is also a rich mix of architectural talent working on the scheme. As well as AHMM, Stanhope invited Morris ＋ Company, MaccreanorLavington, dRMM and Mikhail Riches to contribute new buildings to the masterplan. "It's very important," says Shaw. "It's also a lot of extra work and management because you are dealing with passionate and opinionated people." The result, however, is an eclectic mix of space and form that determines the character and quality of the city. "We are very analytical about the design, and very hands-on," says Shaw. "It's about the space around the buildings. We built the fabric in such a way that it gives the community every chance to be successful."

Opposite page: although a new building, the façade of 2 Television Centre pays respect to the BBC office building which stood on the site previously.

Below: angled bridges on each floor of the new 2 Television Centre building cross over the nine-storey atrium. The walls are board-marked concrete.

Opposite page: the ground floor reception with bridges above.

Looking upwards through the 2 Television Centre atrium. The bridges cross dramatically at each floor, and an enormous skylight allows light to pour into the nine-storey space, reaching all the way down to the reception.

Soft focus

Gillespies, the London-based firm of landscape specialists, came on board the project right at the beginning. The firm had collaborated with AHMM before and became closely involved in the initial planning application, shaping the landscape design around the repurposed footprint of the Television Centre buildings. "We had a certain respect so as not to overwhelm the original building," says the partner leading the project, Stephen Richards, "but it was also a major shift from being a closed, gated environment." The new landscaping is an essential part of tying Television Centre into the wider masterplan in the W12 area. "We also had to accommodate a new connection to Hammersmith Park," Richards explains, noting that the "rich history" of White City was carefully and intensively researched. "You can sometimes get overwhelmed by the history. We had a lot of discussions about the heritage of landscape. There are strong threshold conditions, with a grove of pin oaks at the front of the site, which remove you from the main road."

Gillespies have combined their comprehensive knowledge of planting and trees with a well-developed understanding of how landscape influences a sense of place and how people move through outdoor areas. The most important part of the landscaping is the new piazza fronting Wood Lane, previously a windswept tarmac 'funnel' that was off-limits to all but guests. "It's hard to remember that this was once a private space," says Paul Monaghan.

Today, the idiosyncratic shape is exploited to direct views and visitors towards the entrance of the Helios, overlooked by the logo and famous 'atomic dots' on the wall of the adjoining television studios. "The design evolved over time, starting with a single, triangular piazza to a more complex series of spaces," Richards says, explaining how visitors ascend a series of terraces to a more intimate space at the top, closest to the apartments. This added granularity is enhanced by the fact that each terrace has a distinctive character, progressing to the free planting and winding layout of the one closest to Television Centre, which forms a little oasis of greenery that residents and visitors can hide themselves in. "There's a sense of progression," says Richards. "You go through trees and ultimately enter the circular courtyard through columns. We wanted the terraces to be bold and meet the graphics of the existing building." The Helios courtyard itself has been given a very simple treatment, "taking a cue from the circular forms".

Opposite page: planting in the public forecourt, overlooked by the famous 'atomic dots' of Studio 1. The forecourt is divided into three tiers, ascending to this more intimate garden at the top, which leads to the Helios colonnade and courtyard.

Above: the top and middle tiers of landscaping in the public forecourt, with 2 Television Centre behind. Cafés and restaurants line the south-facing terrace, and generous outdoor seating ensures the space is well used by residents and the public alike.

Opposite page: wildflowers and silver birch trees in the curved garden that runs between the Helios and Crescent. This calmer space offers respite for residents and has been planted to be enjoyable all year round.

Looking down from the Helios
reveals the distinctive tiers designed
by Gillespies. The uppermost
space is an intimate garden, whilst
the lowest tier is paved and hosts
different events throughout the year.

Above: details from the bespoke
concrete planters and benches that
weave throughout the forecourt.

Opposite page: the Helios fountain
is raised above a new staircase that
descends to the basement gym.

The landscaping has been designed to go hand in hand with the elevation treatments and the materials chosen to signal the shift from public-facing spaces to private ones, with natural stone replacing the old tarmac drop-off point and high-specification pre-cast concrete in the circular courtyard. Colour, proportion and change of grain have all been carefully researched.

"To endure you need to have a very high specification," says Richards. "Landscaping has undergone a real renaissance in the last decade or so as to what it can do for the identity of a place. Well-considered and well-maintained landscape really resonates with people."

Television Centre creates a new oasis away from Wood Lane, with trees mitigating the traffic and clear landscaping that pinpoints a new pedestrian route through to Hammersmith Park. Over a hundred years after this area was synonymous with leisure and spectacle, White City is once again a destination. "When I go there now it feels like the building has existed for a while," says Paul Monaghan. "There's a continuity, partly because television is still made here, but also because Soho House and other tenants create life throughout the day. It has a ready-made community – it really feels part of that area of London. The opportunity to create so much new public realm is rare in London, but we've also ensured the interiors are as strong as the exteriors."

London's layers of history have been stitched into a thoroughly modern fabric, with the city's eclectic mix of cultures, occupations and diversions crystallised together in a fine example of contemporary place-making.

The future of London W12

London is a fast-changing city. The skyline you see today from the penthouses and roof terraces of Television Centre will have rewritten itself within the decade, and then again once another ten years go by. At the time of writing, around five hundred new towers were gearing up for construction within Central London, creating new clusters and centres, ensuring that familiar silhouettes will be joined by new shapes, some proudly iconic, others simply jostling for attention in an increasingly crowded field.

The story of twenty-first-century London has been punctuated by developments that endeavour to accommodate our changing ways of working, living, consuming and being entertained. The city has always been characterised by continual change, from the inexorable transformation of the rural into the suburban and then the urban. Two centuries ago, the fields, farms and villages of Shepherd's Bush were waypoints on the road to Acton, Ealing and beyond, far from the noise and pollution of the City and Westminster. The coming of the railways and the massive transformations wrought by everything from the Olympics to international exhibitions and enormous shopping centres has all but scrubbed the land clean of its original uses, many times over.

Development projects are akin to taking part in a city-wide jigsaw, hoping that your neighbours will have a piece of the puzzle that fits alongside your own. Sometimes it works, sometimes not so much. It's a delicate task to inject White City – an area that's known both for television production and its deprived community – with a development consisting of penthouse apartments and a Soho House members' club. But when it comes to entire swathes of an area like White City going through a near-simultaneous evolution, Television Centre has highlighted the value of co-operation, from Stanhope's ongoing involvement with surrounding developments through to AHMM's invitation of contemporary British architects to bring variety and character to the new buildings.

Ultimately, this is still the beginning. The next decade will see more change in the streets of White City than the district has seen since the heady days of the International Exhibitions as the area undergoes its many-staged journey from farmland to showground, to broadcast epicentre, to a lively new neighbourhood. A second stage of construction will bring more office and residential buildings to Television Centre. The trees will eventually mature, creating shade and a buffer between the building's façade and Wood Lane. The verdant landscaping that has done so much to blur the boundaries between public and private space, with shaded paths and walkways between the new buildings, will continue to grow.

W12's renaissance will hopefully remain true to the spirit of the original BBC Television Centre, a building that unified the country's nascent broadcasting talent and created a truly world-leading industry. Modern media is hugely fragmented, but the television studio retains its magnetic appeal, drawing creative talent from around the globe to this familiar corner of the city. New visions will be shaped on the nearby campuses of Imperial College and the Royal College of Art, while the many creative businesses on the site shape the products, services and entertainment of tomorrow.

Imperial College will increasingly become a new force for the area, extending to both sides of the A40. A host of life sciences companies will move to be within close proximity of the institution, creating what some predict will be a new knowledge cluster in West London. But this will be felt outside of the labs, too, on street level. The new campus will bring with it the bustle of more restaurants, retail and residences.

The new homes will increase the permanent population of White City, all of whom are due to benefit from London's ongoing public transport revolution. HS2 and Crossrail 2 will ultimately join the new Elizabeth Line, projected to open December 2019, to transform east–west movement through the capital. White City is effectively just four stops from nearly £100 billion of new transport investment. Other nearby developments include Old Oak Common near Wormwood Scrubs, home to a proposed intersection between HS2 and the Elizabeth Line. A 1,600-acre former goods yard will be transformed into a new city district, with two new tube stations and a population of around 60,000, 15 times more than at present.

Right: crowds waiting patiently to be in the audience for a live studio recording at Television Centre, September 2018.

Opposite page: an aerial photograph of Television Centre from early 2019 shows the completed site. Residents have moved in, restaurants have opened, and television programmes are being made here once again. Across Wood Lane, more homes are under construction as development continues throughout the area.

It will be a noisy few years for White City. With every ambitious new development scheme comes the staccato roar of construction. The bulldozers and cranes will move through the area patch by patch, phase by phase. The development jigsaw puzzle will unfold across this expansive stretch of London – some pieces a natural fit alongside one another, ill-fitting pieces invariably watered down by stakeholders and budgets, while other pieces will become a blueprint for a more walkable, liveable and sociable society.

In a way, the new White City is emblematic of modern London. Self-contained yet also utterly global, it has Television Centre's mix of modernist heritage, contemporary design and international reach at its heart. White City will probably never stand still. Like the rest of the capital, it thrives on change. Just as it has done for over 60 years, Television Centre continues to broadcast a message that inspires, encourages and welcomes – a testament to the success of a mixed-use development that has always looked to the future without ignoring its past.

London W12:
White City timeline

1891
Wormwood Scrubs
prison opens

1895
The Empire of India Exhibition
is held in Earls Court

1907
Construction of the Olympic
Stadium begins

1908
London hosts the
Games of the IV Olympiad

1910
The Japan-British
Exhibition

1911
The Coronation
Exhibition

1927
The British Broadcasting
Corporation is established

1932
Broadcasting House
is completed

1949
Graham Dawbarn is appointed
to design the new BBC HQ

1949
Dawbarn draws his
'question mark' design

1900

Shepherd's Bush
station opens

1903

Shepherd's Bush
Empire opens

1908

The area receives its
new name: White City

1908

The Franco-British
Exhibition

1912

The Latin-British
Exhibition

1914

The Anglo-American
Exhibition

1936

The BBC begins
television transmissions

1945

The White City housing
estate is completed

1950

Construction of
Television Centre begins

1951

The Festival of Britain
is held in London

1953

The BBC purchases the Shepherd's Bush Empire

1954

The Scenery Block is completed

1970

The Westway is opened

1974

The first Blue Peter Garden is completed

1991

The BBC's Lime Grove studios are closed

1998

Stage 6, the BBC's final addition, is completed

2009

Television Centre is Grade II listed

2011

The BBC opens MediaCity in Salford

2013

Broadcasting House renovations are completed

2013

The BBC vacates Television Centre

1956

The Canteen Block
is completed

1960

Television Centre is
officially opened

1985

White City Stadium
is demolished

1990

The BBC's White City building
replaces the stadium

2007

The BBC announces plans
to sell Television Centre

2008

Westfield London
opens

2011

Television Centre is
put up for sale

2012

Sale is agreed to Stanhope
and its development partners

2014

Demolition and
construction begins

2018

Television Centre is
officially re-opened

Thank you

The author and publisher would like to thank everyone involved in helping to make this book a reality, in particular:

Peter Allen, Alistair Shaw, Ron German, Charles Walford and Finn Nixon
Stanhope

Paul Monaghan, Susie le Good, Hazel Joseph and Alex Turner
AHMM

Robert Seatter
BBC History

Karen Meachen and David Simms
BBC Studios

Stephen Richards
Gillespies

Anna Danby
Artifice Press

Ben Dale, Joy Nazzari, Patrick Eley, Tim George and Zoë Barrett
dn&co.

Michael Eaton, Jonathan Bell, Lee Mawdsley, Guy Archard

Photography and image credits

Lee Mawdsley
Front cover, 03, 06, 08–11, 13, 14–19, 85, 97–127, 146–159, 162–167, 170–171, 176, 178–208, 210, 212–215, 220–221, 222, 234, back cover

GG Archard
130, 160–161, 168–169, 172–173, 211, 216–219, 223

Mike O'Dwyer
12, 94–95, 221, 226

Ben Dale
174–175

Kate Peters
129, 145

Jason Hawkes
227

Chris Floyd
239

—

BBC Photo Library
54, 56–63, 64, 66–74, 78–83, 132, 139, 238

Allford Hall Monaghan Morris
133–144

Getty Images
21, 22–37, 39, 42–44, 46–47, 49–53, 65, 76–77, 88–93, 228

London Transport Museum collection
40–41, 93

Alamy
32, 45, 89

Hammersmith & Fulham council archives
38–39

Note: the two drawings on page 55 are uncredited.
Every attempt was made to find the author of these images.

Colophon

© 2019 Artifice Press Limited. All rights reserved.

Artifice Press Limited
81 Rivington Street, London, EC2A 3AY
United Kingdom

+44 (0)20 8371 4000
office@artificeonline.com
www.artificeonline.com

Written by: Jonathan Bell
Designed by: dn&co.
Creative director: Patrick Eley
Designer: Tim George
Project manager: Zoë Barrett
Historical image research: Tim George
Sub editor: Justin Lewis
Contributing editor: Elli Stuhler

British Library in Cataloguing Data. A CIP record for
this book is available from the British Library.

ISBN 978-1-911339-16-8

Printed in the United Kingdom by CPi Colour.

Sir David Attenborough, 1967

Sir David Attenborough, 2018